HOMETOWN ALBUM

by Harriet Fletcher Fisher

PUBLISHED BY
LYNDON HISTORICAL SOCIETY

PUBLISHED BY LYNDON HISTORICAL SOCIETY,
LYNDON, VERMONT

COPYRIGHT © 1995 BY HARRIET FLETCHER FISHER

ISBN 1-56715-024-1
LIBRARY OF CONGRESS CATALOG CARD NO. 95-077336

Front cover photo:
Crowds lined Main Street to watch the horse races. Date of photo not known.

Back cover photo:
The Farm, c. 1950. Cows were in the field for fall feeding.
(Photo by Calvin Chester).

Printed and Bound in the United States of America by
ACADEMY BOOKS
Rutland, Vermont

This book is dedicated to
the memory of my father and mother,
Earl and Emma Fletcher,
who gave me a good life on the farm
and what the village offered as well.

It is also dedicated to my lifelong
"village" friend, Patricia Riley Leslie,
who encouraged me to "collect"
some of my writings into this book.

Table of Contents

PART II: VILLAGE LIFE

Introduction

THIS IS NOT AN AUTOBIOGRAPHY. It is really the biography of an era. The intent is to tell what it was like growing up in that era. I feel fortunate that I lived on a farm with village opportunities nearby.

Our farm land ran down close to the village limits, and the farmhouse itself was only a mile from Lyndonville. We went "down street," or "down town," or to the "Ville." Lyndonville itself is not a town, but is a village in the town of Lyndon.

Though I went to a one-room district school, I knew a lot of the "kids" at the Ville, so when I went to high school at Lyndon Institute there were many fellow students I already knew and it was fun to get acquainted with others.

My brother, Gordon Dana Fletcher, and I got along great, perhaps because he was almost four years younger than I. I remember the day he was born. My father and I were in the kitchen and he told me I had a baby brother. My father said, his eyes all atwinkle, "Hear him cry!" My brother died at Willoughby Lake when he was thirteen years old.

I became interested in Vermont history when I was listening to Mary Pearl's radio program while I was doing housework after my kids went to school. The program promoted Maltex cereal, then made in Burlington. One week Mary Pearl posed questions about Vermont and offered a prize to the first one who would send in the correct answers.

I was so fascinated trying to find the answers that the first thing I knew I had become an avid reader of Vermont history. School superintendent Urban Wakefield found some discarded Vermont history school books for me, and I started collecting Vermont books. I took Graham Newell's Vermont History course at Lyndon State College.

Out of the blue I remembered a shoebox full of post cards that I had stashed on a closet shelf several years before. When I visited my aunt and uncle in St. Johnsbury, Uncle Charles and I would sit on the carpet and build post card villages. I had brought the shoebox home for sentimental reasons when Aunt Carrie had to go to a nursing home many years after Uncle Charles died. That box of post cards sparked my interest in old photos and local history and has been an invaluable resource.

Most of the writings in this book have been rewritten or adapted from my articles that have appeared in various papers, such as *The Burlington Free Press*, *The Caledonian-Record*, *The Chronicle* (Barton), *The Newport Daily Express*, *The Weekly News* (Lyndonville), and *The Lyndon Independent*.

This book is a collection of what it was like here in Vermont when I was growing up. It was a different era, the era I want to relate—not to live in the past, but to record some of that era.

Dad bringing in a load of hay with Pat and Jerry.

The barnyard gate

One of our earlier cars

Farm Life

Ma and Dad and new car. Number plate says 1929. The old granary got a new roof and was used for storing sap buckets, outdated farm implements, and even an old hand-cranked washing machine. It was a wonderful rainy-day playhouse for Gordon and me.

PHOTO BY AUTHOR

Left photo: Gordon Dana Fletcher, born March 4, 1922. The kitchen stove was good for cooking and for keeping a baby brother warm. At right, the Farm gate.

The Art of Coping

MANY PEOPLE from other states have written humorous and interesting books about how they coped with Vermont winters, wild animals, wild land, selectmen, carpenters, plumbers, town characters and unexpected situations. For instance, buying a hillside home in summer, then later finding out what it was like living there in winter, could dish up some surprises.

Native-born Vermonters coped with such things all their lives. Take winter for instance. We coped by wearing long-legged drawers wrapped smartly around the ankles and the stockings pulled carefully and smo-o-o-thly over them. Sometimes, when one sat down, a corner button hole on the back flap of the long drawers would get a terrific pull and stretch, or the button would pop off, letting cool winter breezes seep through the outer clothing to the bare spot. We needed these drawers indoors and out. It was drafty in those days.

We drank water without chlorine and our rumps were not used for a doctor's dart board. We were exposed to all kinds of germs and got immune on our own to just about everything. We fell out of apple trees, walked to school in snow knee deep, or waist high, and when the snow roller came to roll the roads we had the most wonderful sliding track. No matter how high our boots were we got them full of water when this all turned to slush in the spring. It was wonderful stuff to play in.

A snow roller, back view, on display at Orleans County Fair, 1994. The men sat in the wagon seat seen on top.

We slept in the heavenly warmth of a feather mattress that enfolded us, and with a hot water bottle at our feet, we were nested cozily in our beds. No one can imagine the thrill of getting dressed by a hot woodstove until one backs a bare bottom against it, especially when a letter "O" from the word "Glenwood" is branded on one's rump.

We cleared out our systems with a rousing cold once each winter and when green vegetable time came around we got another cleaning out with a 24-hour "summer complaint." We put court plaster on our cuts, salve on our burns, and cold cloths on our sore throats. We learned about the good and evil of the world by reading about giants, fairies, and elves—and the Bible.

We knew life was not always good when big boys bullied little children and we knew about selfishness when some of the other children demanded and always got the new books at school and we got the marked and ragged ones. We knew about illness when we got whooping cough and we knew about fear when the district nurse gagged us with wooden sticks and told us our tonsils looked bad and to have our mothers take us to the doctor. Every time my mother took me, Dr. Cheney always said, "Well, they look all right to me."

War was a little less remote than just words in the history books when we saw a Revolutionary War musket in our attic, along with our great-uncle's Civil War uniform, and photographs of two uncles in World War I uniforms.

Our summer joys were Sunday afternoon drives in THE CAR, wading in the brook, jumping in the hay mow from 30-foot high beams in the barn; reading a book up in a leafy maple tree.

THE CAR—not the roadster with the rumble seat removed and replaced with a home-built body in which my father took milk to the creamery—was a big seven-passenger Hudson with two jump seats. Often in the summer, the car was filled with friends and/or relatives for a Sunday spin and picnic.

Our summer fears were getting one's mouths sewed up by the flying "darning needle" if one swore, as some playmate would have us believe (I didn't test it out); or getting blood suckers attached to our legs if we waded in the muddy part of the brook (I never saw one), a blood sucker, that is. Another thing—some playmates would have us believe that if we drank milk after eating chokecherries, we would get sick. I didn't test that out either.

If all this sounds like a corny childhood, it probably was, but it must be remembered it was lived with zest and eagerness and we didn't know any better but to have fun, cry when we got hurt, or get mad when somebody picked on the little kids. Security was a strip of court plaster and rosebud salve applied by a mom or dad. Bliss was my father saying, "Want to go with me? Get your coat."

My "NEK" of the Woods

H OW MANY people today, I wonder, know that Vermont once had five Congressional districts. The counties, Caledonia, Essex, and Orleans, now known as the Northeast Kingdom, was the Fifth Congressional District. It was represented from 1837 to 1841 when Martin Van Buren was president, by my great grand uncle, Isaac Fletcher, a lawyer, in Lyndon (Corner) since 1811.

In the mid 1940s a group of people from Caledonia, Essex and Orleans counties planned ways to interest people who lived in New Jersey, Massachusetts, Connecticut and other states, to visit northeastern Vermont, buy northeastern Vermont-made products and move onto northeastern lands.

It was foreseen as a way to help the economy and the grand lists so Vermonters would not have to move to New Jersey, Massachusetts, Connecticut and other states for heftier paychecks and a "better way of life."

Some people believe that Aiken used the name Northeast Kingdom when he was Governor of Vermont (1937-1941). He may have, but it really caught on after he used it at a meeting of the Northeastern Vermont Development in 1949.

An article, "Northeast Kingdom" by Wallace Gilpin who published *The Newport Daily Express*, appeared in the Summer 1950 issue of *Vermont Life*. He wrote: "The name [Northeast Kingdom] was given Caledonia, Essex and Orleans counties

A little corner of the Northeast Kingdom. Fletcher Farm buildings, center.

by United States Senator George D. Aiken, former governor of Vermont, in an address at Lyndonville last November."

In 1968, I wrote a letter to Senator George D. Aiken for some kind of verification. This is from his reply: "When I named the Northeast Kingdom years ago, it seemed appropriate because this area obviously held a tremendous potential for development of a prosperous economy based on a wide use of healthy outdoor recreation."

In time, the name Northeast Kingdom became famous. Well, maybe not famous, at least for a while. Around 1960 I visited the beautiful Coolidge State Park at Plymouth. At the Coolidge homestead I signed the guest register with Lyndonville as my address. The attendant turned the book around and repeated the name "Lyndonville" in a rather questioning manner. Thinking to enlighten her I said," Yes, I'm from the Northeast Kingdom." This confounded the situation for she eyed me even more questioningly as though I should be wearing a sari or a costume native to some exotic kingdom. I just shrugged and said to myself, "Well, she's not a Vermonter."

Though the Northeast Kingdom is not an exotic land, it has its own beauty through four seasons—usually white winter, green summer, brilliant fall and misty spring. Some people add "mud season," but we take it in stride with spring—or maybe not in stride, maybe more like in slog, but mud can be a sign of spring.

The Northeast Kingdom, once remote, is now easily accessible via Interstate 91. Housing developments, throughways, paved roads have changed the scenery. Yet there is much natural beauty left—trees, grass, parks, even a fountain or two. There are still some old homes with pleasing lines, picturesque New England churches and residential village streets laid out in neat rows.

Today's goals of preserving some of the best of the old, adapting older buildings to new uses, and well thought out developments, can be a happy medium needed for keeping the Northeast Kingdom a desirable and pleasing place to live.

The name Northeast Kingdom really did catch on and people now know what it is, even when it is abbreviated to "NEK." People from New Jersey, Massachusetts, Connecticut and other states really like our NEK of the woods and have moved onto former farms and many places that Vermonters left a number of years ago to work in New Jersey, Massachusetts, Connecticut and other states.

Massachusetts and Connecticut folk were moving into southern Vermont before the Revolutionary War, not the least of these being Ethan Allen, a "Conn." man from Litchfield. After that war, some of these folks reached the area now known as the Northeast Kingdom. Early settlers from New Hampshire and Rhode Island came also. A few towns in Caledonia County were settled by immigrants directly from Scotland.

Politically speaking, the NEK was once a Republican stronghold and a jumping off place for Democrats. Republican candidates for state offices did not need to visit these three strong Republican counties and there was nothing to be gained for Democrats to enter this Republican bailiwick. Nowadays

Democratic candidates step boldly and bravely into the Northeast Kingdom and the Republicans have to concede them equal time, sometimes even some of the offices.

Y-up, even native-born Northeast Kingdom inhabitants have not lived here all our lives—yet—but we're working on it.

ONION; GARLIC
Genus (*Allium*)

The various species belonging to this genus are very strongly scented, pungent herbs growing from a coated bulb.

(A) WILD LEEK; WILD ONION (*Allium tricoccum*) is a woodland plant blooming in May and June. The flowers are in an umbel at the top of a scape 6 to 20 in. high. The flower perianth is divided into six greenish-white sepals. The leaves are oblong-lance-shaped, pointed at both ends, on long petioles from the bulbous root, but usually withering before the flowers appear. Found from N. B. to Minn. and southward.

(B) WILD GARLIC (*Allium canadense*) has few purplish 6-parted flowers on slender pedicels from a cluster of bulblets at the top of a scape 10 to 24 in. high. The leaves are grass-like, sheathing the stem above the fibrous bulb. Flowers in May and June in moist meadows, from N. B. to Mich. and southward.

A wild leek, from a flower book[1] I had since I was a little girl.

[1]Charles A. Reed, *Flower Guide, Wild Flowers East of the Rockies* (Worcester, MA: Doubleday, Page & Co., 1907)

Food

OOD THAT NEEDED to be kept cool was put in the pantry with the doors closed so there was very little heat in there during the winter. In summer it was put in the cool stone-walled and cemented-floor cellar.

No one worried much about the food they ate. Saturated fat, cholesterol, and these scary things were not known then, at least in our world. The food was pure and natural all on its own. When my mother was planning to make a whipped-cream cake for dinner, or jello that really tasted like fruit, or one of her chocolate puddings, my father took a container and a ladle to the milkhouse before he took the cans to the creamery and scooped off some of the rich cream for my mother to whip.

Dinner was at noon on the farm; in fact, people in the village had dinner at noon too. There might be dried beef and milk gravy, or salt pork fried crisp with milk gravy or beef or pork, (chicken was usually a Sunday dinner), with potatoes, vegetables, pickles and so on. Dessert was usually pie or cake. Cookies and puddings, or sauce, such as rhubarb, were usually supper desserts.

We were slim just the same. I was so skinny that people would ask my mother if I was all right because I was so thin. She always answered, "Well, she is never sick."

We raised our own hogs and chickens. I guess we had beef too, but you didn't kill a milk cow. My mother bought beef

9

occasionally from the traveling meat or grocery cart that came around at regular intervals, or at the meat market in the Ville.

My father smoked our hams and bacon. His "smokehouse" was a large wooden box affair with a door, and a smoke hole on top. When it was smoking time, he hauled it out of storage, put in in the middle of the yard, so it would not be near any buildings in case it caught fire—it never did. After the hams and bacon had been pickled in brine for weeks, he hung them over pans filled with smoldering corn cobs.

My father and I made sausage. We usually did it an evening after he finished chores. My mother would go downstreet and visit with some friends and leave Dad and I to our project. Dad ground the pork and mixed in the proper spices while I sewed up some bags on the sewing machine. We would mix, taste, mix and taste, until we got it right, then Dad would say, "I think we ought to try a little, don't you?" Whereby we got out a frying pan and "fried a little." It was really good but of course the sausage was better after it had time to age some.

Chicken pie, or roast chicken, was a holiday or a Sunday dinner. My mother put a hen that was not laying well in a coop and fattened it with corn. She even cut off the hen's head if Dad was not right around when she needed to get it ready. After plucking it with my help,—Yuk!—she took a rimmer off the stove, held the bird by the legs and skipped it across the flames to singe off the hairs left under the feathers. Some had pinfeathers that had to be pulled out with pliers.

When Ma made pickles she set a crock on a stool in a corner by the kitchen cabinet where they would sit in the brine for a specified number of days. She often made those little cucumber pickles. Gordon and I, when we thought no one was looking, picked a cucumber out of the brine, sucked off that salty liquid and dropped the cucumber back in the brine. Ma would have had a fit if she had caught us. I wonder if perhaps she did see us sometimes but pretended she didn't.

Of course amidst canning, preserving, and pickling, there were apples to peel, slice and dry. Dried apple pie was a favorite of both my mother and father. My mother was particularly fond of the Duchess tree in our small orchard back of the house. The Duchess apples were so good for pies and applesauce. We really felt bad when that old tree winter-killed in the severe winter of 1933-34.

Ma liked the doughnuts when they were right out of the kettle and still crispy. When she finished frying them she poured herself a cup of coffee or a glass of milk and sat down to enjoy two doughnuts. She never ate another one until she fried another batch. It was like the chocolate cake. She ate one piece when it was first put on the table and never touched another piece until she made the next one.

We were on our own for Sunday supper, the only meal from which my mother took a "vacation." In winter, Dad sent me up to the kitchen chamber to get a few ears from the braids of popcorn hanging from the ceiling.[2] I shelled them while he fired up the stove to red hot. When the popcorn was in the wire popper, he grinned at me as he stepped outside with the popper, "to shake the snow out."[3]

Dad saved out a bowl of popcorn before he put the salt and butter on the rest. His supper was the bowl of popcorn and milk. I didn't much care for that, but loved the popcorn with the salt and butter. My mother often made corn meal mush for her Sunday night supper, but Dad and I didn't go for that too much.

Gordon and I, and maybe some of our playmates ate grain out of the grain bin in the barn, by scooping some into our hands

---

[2] The husks of ears of corn were pulled back. Three ears were braided by the husks, adding more as the braid grew. These hung in a warm place to dry.

[3] The "snow" was little white hulls that came off the cob with the shucking of the corn from the ears.

and taking a few laps. There were different flavors, some had molasses, and none of them had any other additives.

We found lots of things to eat outdoors. We could stash the saltshake, as we called it, in our pockets for things like a stalk of rhubarb or green apples. We strapped jars around our waists and climbed bird (also known as pin) cherry trees. We ate chokecherries too.

We picked the bitter-tasting sorrel leaves to eat, sucked the ends off honeysuckle blossoms and found checkerberries down by the brook. We liked to chew checkerberry leaves as well.

I guess the payoff for outdoor provisions, was the time Gordon and I went up in the sugar woods. We found some leeks, pulled them up, took off that outer skin and ate quite a bunch of them. When we got home and walked into the house Ma made us go right back out. She didn't let us back in for quite a while—not until the smell kind of wore off. Leeks are much stronger than onions, but oh, so good!

The Creamery

E VER SINCE I was very small and later if it wasn't a school day my father would say, "Want to go to the creamery with me?" I'd climb in the roadster. He had taken the rumble seat out and replaced it with a wooden body he had built to hold the milk cans. I learned quite a bit of what the creamery was about.

The creamery was just north of Lyndonville by the Passumpsic River. Farmers, or someone bringing in cans of milk for farmers, backed their pickups, trucks, or horse drawn rigs up to the platform and got out to set the cans on a steel roller that pulled the cans inside through a door just big enough for the cans. That was because in winter the less opening there was the warmer it stayed inside. Shortly, they returned through another small door all steamy from being scalded. The cans were marked with numbers so each farmer or deliverer got the same cans back. If there were several people there at the same time, they had to wait their turn to get to the platform. Some farmers got so they knew about when to expect some of the big trucks and tried to get there before.

Sometimes we went down back after unloading the milk to get a pound of butter or a small tub of cottage cheese. The butter was wrapped in parchment-like paper and put in a white

Ozzie Gilman drove this Speedwell Farms truck.

box with a pink clover on it. The butter and cheese were made right there at the creamery.

In 1890, W. Irving Powers, clerk and treasurer of Theodore N. Vail's Speedwell Farms, organized the Lyndonville Creamery and was its general manager. He was also president of the Lyndonville Board of Trade, the forerunner of the Chamber of Commerce. The creamery provided an outlet for milk from Theodore N. Vail's more than 100 thoroughbred cows at Speedwell Farms. Milk and cream from other dairies were handled here too. In time even small farmers from Lyndon and area towns made their living by sending or taking their milk to this creamery.

The creamery association owned and operated a chain of fourteen creameries in Vermont and New Hampshire with a large branch near Boston for handling its own products.

This was a successful separator creamery, the first in this area. Butter made there in the morning was shipped by rail in ice chests and reached restaurants and hotels in Boston by

The Creamery, Lyndonville, Vermont

evening meal time. Later, milk, butter and cheese were shipped by refrigerated trucks.

From 1933 to 1938, Osmore (Ozzie) Gilman was one of several who drove a Speedwell Farms refrigerated truck from the creamery, to Watertown, Massachusetts. Back then it was a six- or seven-hour drive to cover the 200 miles. The drivers worked seven days a week including holidays—to Massachusetts one day, back the next.

The truck had a 125 gallon tank for milk. Doors on the side opened where milk jugs holding 85 pounds were carried. Cheese was carried in the back. The creamery made cheese with olives, cheese with chives, cottage cheese and butter. The skim milk from the creamery cheese and butter making was fed to pigs kept in a piggery back of the creamery.

The buildings are gone except the one that was the office. It was moved further from the road and remodeled into what became the Town and Country Restaurant. It has again been moved and remodeled and for a while was the Highwater Cafe. The building is not in use at present.

Two Horse Power

T HE PHOTO of Jerry and Major was taken one morning while I was walking crosslots through the pasture on my way to work at the Lyndonville Electric Plant office, then located in the village hall (also called Music Hall), where the post office is now. The horses must have been in the pasture between jobs.

We did not have a carriage horse because we had a roadster with the rumble seat removed and made into a small "pickup," and we had a touring car that I especially remember when I was small because of some wonderful Sunday trips. Dad took the milk to the creamery in the roadster "pickup." In winter, he paid a neighbor to take it with his and others on a horse-drawn sled in the days before roads were plowed so well that we could drive on them most of the winter.

In mud time, if the ground froze in the night Dad did his milking early so he could take the milking from the night before and the morning milking to the creamery in the "pickup" while the roads were still frozen. I think the same neighbor stopped for the milk with his horse-drawn vehicle if the roads were too bad for the roadster.

Horses worked in the woods in winter snaking out logs to be cut for fire-wood, or taken to Wetherbee's Mill to be sawed into lumber. While Dad was in the mill on business, my brother and I would play in the mill yard.

PHOTO BY AUTHOR

Jerry and Major, 1940.

Sometimes we found a spinning top that had been discarded because it was imperfect. Wetherbee not only sawed lumber, but made many things in the shop, such as chair rungs candlepins, and their famous spinning tops.

Sometimes the logging activity made paths in the sugar woods that did not completely disappear during snow storms so that it was not so hard to break roads for sugaring. The team pulled the sled with the gathering tank from tree to tree so the sap could be poured from the buckets into the tank.

Then this was driven out of the sugar woods and the sap in this tank piped to another huge stationary tank just outside the woods at the top of the hill. This saved the horses from having to draw the full load down hill, and pull the sled and tank back up for the next load of sap, a hard job for the horses even when the gathering tank was empty. At times the tracks could get slippery from use.

The sap in the tank on top of the hill could be released by faucet to run through a pipe to the covered holding tank that was on a platform high on the side of the sugarhouse. From there, the sap could be released as needed into the huge boiling pan.

Farm horses pulled the mowing machine to cut the hay. Later, one of the horses would be hitched to the tedder that tossed and turned the hay over so it would dry thoroughly. This had to be done after a rain, too. When the hay was dry, one of the horses was hitched to the hay rake, also known as a dump rake because when your foot pressed a lever the tines lifted and the hay dropped in a neat row. The row was lengthened by the rake dumping the next load beside the last, forming nice, long winrows so the hired hand with a pitchfork could walk along the winrows, making piles that could be lifted to the hay wagon by one person with a pitchfork.

My mother liked driving the horses. Sometimes she mowed hay, one of her favorite things to do on the farm even though she didn't necessarily have to. She often drove the hay rake, too. She liked working outdoors.

Extra help was hired during haying because there was a lot more work, and everyone knows you "have to make hay while the sun shines." Men and boys would come asking for haying jobs and Dad usually took on one or two; some came back regularly each summer.

The hay was pitched onto the hay wagon with someone on top to place and tromp it down evenly so it wouldn't slide off the wagon on the way to the barn. At the barn, one horse was unhitched so he could pull the horse-fork. With one man on the load to set the horse-fork into the hay and one man up in the mow, the horse walked along led by someone, often my mother, to pull the horsefork up into the barn. When the forkful of hay reached the top of the barn and started on the track over the mow, someone called "Whoa!" and the man in the mow yanked the rope to open the fork and release the hay. Then

Dad on the dump rake, date not known. Back then, they kept three horses.

he would send the fork back and mow[1] away the hay while the fork went back to the wagon for more. My brother or I often rode on the back of the horse while he was pulling the horse-fork.

There were many other chores for horses on the farm— pulling cultivators, seeders, carts, sleds, or wagons for carting things to and from.

The last pair of horses on the farm—the Fletcher farm— were dapple grays. Dad more or less kept them as pets after he had all the equipment he needed to work the farm with a tractor.

---

[1]Here the word "mow" is pronounced like "how." It can be a verb or a noun—a mow to put the hay in; or to mow it away—put it in the mow.

Send It Around Again, Please

RECYCLING, something our ancestors did all the time without thinking about it, is a great concern today. Our ancestors weren't thinking "recycling." They were thinking, "Use it up, wear it out, make it do, or do without." Besides, it was just Yankee thrift, and Yankee thrift—recycling—covered just about everything from chicken feed to Great Aunt Abby's dress.

My grandmother "cycled" the chicken feed through her hens. When the hens were through with it, or rather, after it was through the hens, and when Aunt Carrie came to visit, she took some back to St. Johnsbury in an old coffee can. She added water and let it soak in her basement until ready to use, then diluted the liquid even more to water her plants. Her fernery was filled with biggest, healthiest coleuses I ever saw, and her rabbit's foot fern in a jardiniere in the bay window was a beauty.

Even some of the hens were recycled—right into the oven. Of course that put a damper on any further recycling from them! There was one more use though. The wings were excellent for brushing the ashes from the stove hearth.

Sears and Roebuck catalogs became booster chairs for tots, and soapy laundry water became kitchen floor mop water. Corn cobs were carefully dried, and saved for smoking hams and bacon. Of course, Sears Roebuck catalogs and corn cobs had other uses, I understand, in the old outhouse, but we recycled

It was my job to shell the corn and feed it to the hens.

so much we were affluent enough not to have to resort to that harsh treatment.

Great Aunt Abby's dress was washed, taken apart and "turned," because the material was a little brighter on what had been the wrong side. The material was then made into the latest style school dress for the niece. Uncle Charlie's old coat became a jacket for nephew. Thread was carefully pulled from garments being taken apart so if it was still strong it could be used for sewing something else.

Of course we also had clothes from new material, and the leftovers in Grandma's scrap bag were fun to go through on a stormy day when we looked for pieces to make doll clothes.

All the buttons, hooks and eyes were saved for other garments. Grandma's button box was another source for stormy day fun. A child could string the buttons or match the ones alike and learn to count. Some of great uncle's brass buttons from his Civil War uniform were in that box.

There was no plastic. Cans and bottles were not so much of a problem years ago. Many things were purchased from bulk supplies in the store, put into paper bags, or in a basket the shopper brought from home. There was also less packaging and bottles because more food was raised at home, and more dressings, sauces, jams, and jellies were made at home.

What bottles, cans and jars people did buy, when emptied, were cleaned and used for something else. In some cases, when the bottle or jar was not suitable for another use, it could be thrown in one's private dump that might be a hollow in the pasture that needed filling anyway.

No one realized that dumps would some day be a problem. They could be fun. My mother was one who began digging in our old farm dump and found some quite valuable cobalt blue and other bottles buried in the dirt and grass.

To get rid of cardboard packages, such as cereal boxes, we simply burned them in the wood fire in the kitchen or in the furnace in the cellar. A few burned at a time did not create any problem as far as anyone knew, and all people had of those were usually a few at a time.

There was no junk mail to dispose of; newspapers were good for packing things away, for padding under carpets, or for starting fires in the stove.

Conspicuous consumption was not something we thought about very much on the farm. If we got a new car, a new piece of farm machinery, something new for the house, or to wear, it was because we needed it. One of my biggest thrills as a little girl was new shoes. That did not mean that we couldn't have something more of a frivolous nature at times. Christmas and birthdays were special for gifts such as books, sleds, skates, a bracelet, games or other things.

Christmas wrapping and ribbons were stored away in the hall closet upstairs and "recycled" at least one more Christmas. Of course we did not have Scotch tape to stick to the paper then.

Many things were handed down from generation to generation to be used over and over and if this generation doesn't drop it, we can serve a turkey on a beautiful old flow-blue platter that great grandmother had used and cared for because she just didn't go out and buy a new one at the drop of a hat.

And speaking of hats, one could retrim a hat and make it look like new.

These are only a few of the ways people saved and recycled, but it was not necessarily because they were stingy or even that poor—it was just a way of life.

Today, some of the things we can recycle are newspapers, bottles, plastic jugs, tin cans, and more. There are people dealing with problems of recycling more things and how to dispose of unwanted material. We see evidence all the time now of recycled material being made reusable.

A First Memorable Christmas

ONE CHRISTMAS morning many years ago, before the light had beamed into my bedroom window and before I even knew what Christmas was, I awoke to my father's voice as he bent over my bed and said, "Harriet, come with me, I want to show you something."

I got out of bed and followed my father. We made quite a pair, he in his long flannel nightshirt and me in my Dr. Dentons (a fleecy sleeping suit with feet, and a buttoned flap in the back for you-know-what).

We went through a cold bedroom and into the sitting room warmed by the wood stove. He opened another door and we went into the cold front hall. Then he slowly opened the door to the parlor warmed by the wood fire in the "Gold Coin" parlor stove. His manner was mysterious as he leaned over to me and said, "Look!"

What a sight greeted my eyes! There was a Christmas tree all silvery with tinsel and icicles and fragile old-fashioned ornaments of many colors. There were little feathered birds clamped to the branches. A little old fashioned Santa Claus was propped prominently on one branch.

The tree glimmered and shimmered with candlelight, which was reflected in the shiny colored ornaments. The candles were held firmly on the branches in metal holders with strong clasps.

A child in a footed sleeping suit. From an old post card.

He had gotten up early to stoke the fire in the sitting room and built one in the parlor stove so it would be warm too. He lighted the candles and got me up while it was still dark so I would get the full effect of the candlelight on the tree. We had electricity in the house but there were no electric Christmas lights then. The beautiful old ornaments, the tinsel garlands and the hanging silver icicles were trimmings from family Christmas trees of the past. These were carefully kept in boxes on a high shelf in the upstairs hall closet.

Through the years, we used those tinsel garlands until they became tarnished and worn out. The fragile ornaments gradually got broken, though some lasted long enough for my children to put on their Christmas trees. The candleholders and birds are gone and of course, we got electric lights for the tree. I still have the little old-fashioned Santa Claus.

I do not remember what I received for gifts that day I call my first-remembered Christmas. My most vivid memory besides that beautiful tree that my father set up to surprise me was his happy grin and his eyes that twinkled as much as the candles.

Deep mud on "the flats" by Catholic Cemetery.

Knee-Deep in Mud

MUD IS A SURE SIGN of spring, but the problem of the muddy country road has been greatly alleviated over the years. The use of heavy machinery, much graveling and paving has made a difference on many back roads.

The spring of 1935 was an extra bad year for washouts and mud. Mud along the "flat," from what is now the Packing House all the way to where Lyndon Outing Club is now located, made the road impassable for a while, especially that year. One or two washouts just down the road from our house (Fletcher's) were so bad they were more like thigh-deep than knee-deep. Many other roads that year were as bad or worse.

Snow from the rollers, which were not used after the early thirties, was packed down, not pushed out of the road as it is with the big heavy plows now. When the spring thaws came after the rollers had packed the snow all winter, the roads were rivers of slush and water. Road crews did the best with what they had in those days, using shovels to dig ditches to "turn the water" into the culverts and fields.

Children folded the legs of their long underwear around their ankles, pulled on the long cotton stockings and the woolen socks, and put on their shiny new rubber boots. Then they went out to turn the water like the road men and when a good river was rushing along the ditches, they sailed boats, usually made of small sticks and pieces of wood.

29

Top photo: Thigh-deep hole, approaching the farm.

No matter how tall the boots were, somehow the children always managed to get into slush over the tops. When the boots and stockings were removed, the underwear legs drooped soggily around the ankles. The kitchen smelled of hot wool and warm rubber as these articles dried behind the kitchen stove with its wood

PHOTOS BY AUTHOR

Above: Deep mud near bridge over brook. 1935.

fire. There was a certain odor in the mixture of wet wool and feet, probably not found elsewhere.

After the slush and water cleared away somewhat, there were mudholes and washouts. Mud has certain uses though. Birds use it for building nests, pigs use it for a cleansing agent, and children love it for making pies with and tracking in the house. But on the old dirt roads, it was a booby trap for an autombile. Crews could not fix the roads permanently until the spring rains and thaws were over and all the frost was out of the ground.

Very often, a mud hole separated a farmer from his milk market, a housewife from the groceries, a fellow from his girl, and a teacher from her school. Rural schools often planned to have spring vacation whenever mud season arrived.

Cars were higher and heavier, but during mud season no one "owned" the road. A fellow might attempt to drive through the mud to get his date, mire his car up to the running-boards, walk to the house, and sheepishly ask his date's father for help. The father might take the opportunity to tease the fellow a little, but would willingly hitch up the horses and pull the car from the offending hazard.

Sometimes when a cold spell set in and the rutted roads froze, a car would slip into ruts and a car coming the other way might be locked in the same set of ruts. One would sometimes have to back up until it was out of the ruts and wait until the other car got by.

If the temperature did go down to freezing at night, a farmer would plan to get up extra early in the morning to do the chores and get his milk to the creamery before the frozen road started thawing out in the morning sun, and anyway, he had to get back home to gather the sap and start boiling it at the sugarhouse to make maple syrup.

The Art of Crab Apple Dinging

CRAB APPLE DINGING is probably not an art at all, but it took a certain technique to get a crab apple to go dinging through the air. When a playmate's mother asked, "What did you do at Fletchers' today?" the answer might very well be, "We were dinging crab apples."

But the nice red crab apples were off limits for dinging. When these crab apples were cooked just so, the pulp was put into a cloth bag that was hung from a nail under the pantry shelf. The juice would drip out into a big cooking pot. Once I squeezed the bag just a little to see the juice drip out faster, but I was caught doing that and my mother let out a yelp. "Don't do that!" She explained that squeezing the bag would force out traces of the cooked apple and the jelly would come out looking cloudy instead of clear red.

Big plump sour cream cookies had a teaspoonful of red crab apple jelly dropped in the little hollow my mother made in the center of each cookie just before they were popped into the wood stove oven. The cookies baked to a golden hue and the jelly hardly changed its texture in the baking. The cookie rose up around the jelly just enough to hold it firmly. We kids ate around the jelly until the last delicious morsel of cookie included that bit of heavenly crab apple jelly.

Dinging crab apples with my brother and kids from the village who came to play was quite a sport. Someone usually

DRAWING BY ANN WATKINS SOMERS

Dinging Crab Apples.

produced a jackknife for cutting sticks. Seems to me there was a time or two when we had a little difficulty with my mother over using the paring knife. We cut straight sticks from bushes growing beside the road. Dead sticks would not do—they had to have flexibility for dinging. We got a couple of pails and filled them with crab apples found under the tree that produced the kind not good for jelly.

The sticks, stripped of twigs and leaves, were sharpened on one end and the point pushed into a crab apple. With one's arm holding the stick raised in the air and bent at the elbow, a good smart forward snap of the forearm would send a crab apple dinging through the air for a long way. You had to stop your arm at the right point or the crab apple wouldn't ding at all, but land with a thud in front of you. A bend of the wrist could also spoil a ding. You had to keep your wrist stiff and snap your whole forearm. I believe my father showed me the correct way to ding crab apples.

The most fun was taking sides for crab apple fights. Two or three of us climbed up onto the barn roof and two or three on the hen house roof, and we started dinging crab apples at each other.

We must have decided winners by the number of hits, but our aim couldn't have been too accurate because I don't recall getting hurt. It seems that a kid would remember something like that unless the fun of crab apple dinging was more memorable than the pain.

Number, Please

"HELLO, OPERATOR? Number one-three-four ring one-three, please." In 1915, the listing for this number in the telephone directory under Lyndonville, was "J.A. Fletcher, farm, 134-13."

When the telephone rang, it would ring one long ring and three short rings. You had to be sure to say "ring" in place of the hyphen when the operator said, "Number, please," to avoid any misunderstanding of the number desired.

Finding the Fletcher listing in a 1915 telephone directory someone gave me recently brought back memories of the old wall telephone I remember in the 1920s. It may possibly have been the same one in the photo—it looked the same anyway. I think we got our first desk phone sometime in the 1930s.

There were lots of party lines "in the old days" and other rings would have been heard, too. People on the same line could also hear when someone rang for the operator. When someone answered the telephone, they could hear the clicks if others on the party line picked up their receivers to listen in.

The telephones themselves were as good as the batteries in the set. When the batteries were weak, it was hard to hear someone on the telephone. If other people on the party line picked up too, it was even harder to hear.

To get the operator, you had to push in a button with your left hand while you gave the crank a quick short turn with your

*J. A. Fletcher
reading* Youth's
Companion.
Note Telephone.

right hand, then take the receiver off the hook on the left. The
mouth piece was adjustable up or down to suit the height of
the person talking—very convenient.

This 1915 directory was for the subscribers to the Passumpsic Telephone Company connecting with the Bell System in
Newport, Vermont. The towns under the Passumpsic Company listings were all in the three county area that today we
call the Northeast Kingdom. The initial rate for toll calls was
ten cents for the first five minutes.

According to the book, the operator assistance included the
following directory assistance: "If the person to whom you desire
to speak has no telephone, the toll operator will, when feasi-
ble, make an effort to secure a messenger to notify this person
to come to a pay station." How's that for service! There would
have been a small charge in addition to the toll.

To make emergency calls, the subscriber was instructed to
say, "fire emergency" or "police emergency." If you did not know
of a doctor to call, you would say, "Give me a doctor, emergency," and the operator would try to connect you with a
physician.

Newspapers told stories of heroic operators who stayed at

the switchboards during flood and fire—some of them mighty close—and other emergencies in order to put calls through that were vital to the situation, as long as the lines were still working.

Among the Lyndonville advertisements in the 1915 Passumpsic Telephone Company directory, using modest space at the bottom of a page, were (no yellow pages then): D.C. Stevens, insurance; "Hot Stuff," our coal, Stuart & Son; Squires & Lincoln, confectionery, cigars, tobacco; and Stahler's Garage. Familiar names to Lyndon's "old timers."

The Mail Must Go Through

"**N**EITHER SNOW NOR RAIN nor heat nor gloom of night stays these couriers from the swift completion of their appointed rounds." Well, maybe not "swift" in today's age of speed, but no doubt completed, judging from their equipment and animated power.

Herodotus, the Greek historian, wrote the quoted words about the Persian postal system of 500 B.C. The date of the quote is known, but the date of this photo is not. Whenever it was, there were evidently three Rural Free Delivery (RFD) routes out of Lyndonville at the time. Perhaps it was mud season when it would be difficult to drive automobiles.

The post office was for many years located on the corner of Church and Depot Streets. This photo was taken on the Church Street side of the post office at the back door where incoming mail bags were brought in and outgoing mail bags carried out for loading.

The front entrance on Depot Street with its two heavy doors, one opening in, the other opening out, closed themselves by an air pump at the top of each door. Inside the post office was a steam radiator where, on a 20- or 30-below zero winter morning when one's breath froze on turned up coat collars and hair not tucked into the hat, one could stop a few minutes to melt the frost and warm up a bit. This was the halfway point on my two-mile walk between home and Lyndon Institute.

Ready to go. Clarence Batchelder, Harris Allen, Lucius Park.

Lyndonville's first post office was in the Walker Hotel on the corner of Depot and Main streets where the Cobleigh library is now located. On April 13, 1868, the U.S. Post Office Department notified George Walker, the proprietor, that he was appointed postmaster of Lyndonville, ending the discussion on what to call the village. What became Lyndonville was an area that was flourishing because the Connecticut and Passumpsic Rivers Railroad had built their extensive railroad shop operations here, beginning in 1866.

The first official Colonial American postal system was in 1639 in the Massachusetts Bay Colony when Richard Ffayerbanke was given permission by the General Court to receive and dispatch mail at Boston. He was a cousin to the ancestor of the Fairbanks who invented the platform scale in St. Johnsbury.

Mr. Ffayerbanke ran a tavern, making it one of the handiest places for sending or receiving letters. For his service as America's first "postmaster" he was to receive one cent for each letter he handled. This was good money in those days. A penny could buy a loaf of bread.

The first U. S. postage stamps were issued in 1847. Until then, the handler wrote "paid" in the corner of the letter. And in 1896, an advancement in the postal system allowed more people to receive mail with the first Rural Free Delivery in Virginia. This gave farm area people who did not get "to town" very often the opportunity to receive a daily newspaper. The National Grange and other farmers' organizations were credited for getting Congress to provide the money for establishing RFD.

The "completion of appointed rounds" could be very difficult in our areas back in the days of unpaved roads. The mailman on RFD 1, east side of town, was in my earliest memory, Llewellyn (Tass) Eggleston. In winter months he had rubber lags from back wheel to front wheel on each side of his car to help him through the deep snow. Roads were rolled then, but he must have had to go through some snow before the roller got them all rolled. If the snow softened up before the route was finished, a carrier could get stuck.

Alphonse Aubin, who delivered mail to RFD 3, converted a Model A Ford for snow and mud by using caterpillar treads and skis.

The present Lyndonville post office on Broad Street was built in 1960 on the site of the Music or Village Hall that burned in 1954.

This elm tree behind the Fletcher barns was just a "baby" when the Dutch Elm disease was raging.

In Memory of Elms

O NCE THERE WERE ELMS along the streets in Lyndonville. The parks were shaded with these tall regal trees. Elm trees made a handsome archway over most of the length of Main Street. They thrived in farm yards, along country roads, and along the river.

On March 24, 1867, the *Vermont Union* said: "The railroad folks are putting in elm trees on both sides of the streets in this new village (Lyndonville). They will have in a few years, one of the most attractive villages in northern Vermont." They didn't count on future electric poles and wires, automobiles, and Dutch elm disease, but nevertheless the elms, along with maples, were a great part of the beauty of the village years ago.

"Houghton's tree" stood in the center of the small triangular park by the railroad station. Austin Houghton was a Lyndonville trustee and worked to keep the parks nice.

"Houghton's tree" was the talk of the town. There were many people believed it would not live when he planted it and wondered when the funeral for the tree would be held. But in 1885 the paper said: "Houghton's tree is alive and Houghton is happy." Today the station, the park and the elm are all gone. The park became parking spaces, but I remember that wonderful elm.

Some elms are vase shaped, spreading out gradually from the lowest branches, others are formed like umbrellas. Sometimes the term "feather duster" is used instead of "umbrella."

43

Elms attained a heighth from 75 to 100 feet and normally would have lived more than 200 years. Many cities and towns in New England were resplendent with elm trees towering over their buildings, streets, and parks.

Elm was not so valuable for its wood as maple, but it was strong wood used for such things as farm implements, furniture, and boats. It was also used for fuel, although many elms have a stringy quality that makes them hard to split. Indians made rope from the strong fibers in the American elm bark.

In 1972 Elizabeth Walter Nelson was living at Riverside, her maternal ancestral home. She tried to save an elm on the lawn, the one survivor of several her grandfather, Dudley P. Hall, had planted during the landscaping of Riverside built in 1866. The others had succumbed to Dutch elm disease.

The Elm Research Institute (ERI) of Waldrick, New Jersey, is dedicated to the preservation of American Elms. Mrs. Nelson described the survivor and sent photographs. ERI sent her a plaque designating the tree a historic landmark to be honored and preserved for future generations.

The accompanying letter points out the environmental significance of elms: "Their value goes beyond beauty, and their cooling shade actually reduces summer heat 15 to 20 degrees. They help purify the air by utilizing carbon dioxide and liberating oxygen. Trees lining a village street absorb much of the noise from heavy traffic. You are the honored custodian of part of a nation's heritage of beauty."

Mrs. Nelson loved parties and held a ceremonial one for the tree, with the Burklyn Garden Club, Walter Hubbard from the Vermont Historical Society, and other guests. Refreshments included punch served from Riverside antique silver pitchers.

The tree underwent an intravenous type of treatment in the hope of saving it, but in the end the disease proved to have been too far along and the tree did die.

On June 15, 1866, the *Vermont-Union* says that Captain Frank Fletcher "has lined the highway running past his farm with two rows of trees, maple on one side and elm on the other." Some of the maples are still there, but the elms met their ends during the Dutch Elm disease epidemic around fifteen to twenty years ago. In my generation these maples were great for climbing, but elms were already tall before the limbs began and had a majestic quality in their very height, a little awesome to a small child.

In the town of Lyndon there are some live elm trees, particularly along the river banks.

SOUVENIR

Hog Street School,
Lyndonville, Vermont.

Spring Term, 1899.

PRESENTED BY
SADIE E. HOUGHTON, Teacher.

SCHOOL BOARD:
H. W. LYSTER, F. D. SMITH, L. C. TODD.

There Really Was a Hog Street

S OME PEOPLE ASK about Hog Street and if there really was a Hog Street in town. There really was, and a Hog Street School too. Even in recent years one man who built a house on this road, now known as Lily Pond Road, liked the old name of "Hog Street" and used it on his business cards.

'In earlier days, farmers did not have to fence in their hogs. It was said that hogs raised by the people on the road roamed pretty much at will in the days when only an occasional horse and carriage passed by. Hogs didn't usually venture far from their daily rations.

Later Hog Street School was called Shonyo School. In my school days it was the Fletcher School, but the road remained Hog Street. The school building is still there, just up the hill from the current Lyndon Town School, but it is now a private home, and the street has become Lily Pond Road.

I have the old record books of this school dating from 1835 to 1914. They make interesting reading. The neighborhood ran the school. John Dunton who was chosen moderator in 1835, was then living on the property that became the Fletcher family farm. There was a clerk, a collector of rates, and a committee of three. Though called Hog Street School, it was District 14 for the record and town designation.

The meetings were usually held in March and November, to decide on the next term of school, supplying wood, and

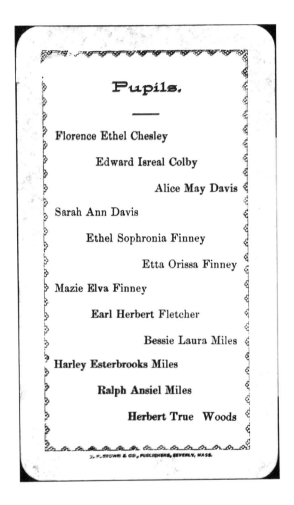

Pupils.

Florence Ethel Chesley

Edward Isreal Colby

Alice May Davis

Sarah Ann Davis

Ethel Sophronia Finney

Etta Orissa Finney

Mazie Elva Finney

Earl Herbert Fletcher

Bessie Laura Miles

Harley Esterbrooks Miles

Ralph Ansiel Miles

Herbert True Woods

J. P. BROWN & CO., PUBLISHERS, BEVERLY, MASS.

making repairs. A few exceptions included voting to build a woodshed, a new roof, a new chimney, and, in one case, a school privy.

At the meetings the "inhabitants" voted on a term of school and voted the rate per "scholar" to raise the funds to pay for same. In 1835, for example, they voted to raise five dollars on the grand list to repair the school house, and buy a record book. Wood was to be furnished at a designated amount "per scholar." A family with two school children, for instance would furnish twice the amount as a family with one. Henry Coburn was to get the wood to make up for anyone who neglected to furnish his share, and he could charge them 70 cents per cord.

The rate each family paid to raise the funds voted, was based on the number of pupils from that family and the amount for for which their property was assessed on the grand list. One list shows it was six cents per child for a term.

In November 1838 one item on the notice was to see if the district would vote to have a female teacher. That article was dismissed at the meeting. One item says: "Voted that the master be boarded round with the scholars." Their fare must have depended on the living and eating habits of each family.

My grandfather, Joseph Fletcher, was the clerk from 1845 to 1859. When they moved to the farm from Hollis, New Hampshire, in 1839, they had five children and two more were born here—seven good reasons for his continued service in one school office or another.

The record books of 1835 to 1893, do not refer to any name for the school at all, but everything is recorded as District School No. 14, until 1859, when it was changed to District School No. 5. Apparently, the school districts were renumbered as the neighborhoods grew and a school was built in yet another neighborhood. Before the Mt. Hunger school was built just off what is now route 114, pupils in that area also came to District School No. 14 on Hog Street.

There is no explanation why the women took over the meeting on March 19, 1881. Mrs. John Allen was voted clerk; Mrs. S. D. Newcomb, collector and also treasurer; and Mrs. Abigail Graves, committee. As clerk, Mrs. John Allen signed the next notice of the meeting to be held a year later, but then the men took the offices again. It can only be presumed that something kept the men away for that one meeting. It would be interesting to know. By that time, the school was running on a yearly, rather than a term basis. It closed for good in 1950.

One-Room School

T HE ROAD WHERE I LIVE was called Hog Street years ago and the school was known as Hog Street when my father went there. For a while it was Shonyo School. By the time I went to school it was Fletcher School and remained so until it closed in 1950 and later became a private home.

Today more than 700 children, kindergarten through eighth grade, go to school in one building, the Lyndon Town School, with many rooms. This is quite different than when all eight grades—no kindergarten then—were in one-room schools in various districts in town. There were also three larger village schools in Lyndonville, Lyndon Center, and Lyndon Corner.

School was from 9 to 4 o'clock. We had two fifteen-minutes recesses, one in the forenoon and one in the afternoon, and an hour at noon when we walked home for dinner. During the darkest weeks of winter, we brought lunch in a dinner pail and had a half hour at noon so we could leave for home at 3:30 before it got too dark—no silly daylight saving time then.

We waded through snow, slush, and mud in turn as the seasons changed. Roads were rolled and the packed snow turned to slush in the spring, making the roads muddy when the slush disappeared. In the spring, we picked wild flowers on the way to school and kept a list on one of the blackboards to see how many different flowers we found.

PHOTO COURTESY IDA WHEELER, TEACHER

Four of the Fletcher School pupils, early 1920s. Harriet Fletcher, Beverly, Russell and Howard Stahler.

During recess, we played blind man's bluff, prisoner's base, baseball, and other games. In winter we played fox and geese in the pasture across the road, or went sliding down the road as long as we could get back before the bell rang. On stormy days, we stayed in at recess or noon time to read or draw, or sing around the old pump organ. I was the only one in school that had had piano lessons so I played the organ. Part of the morning ritual was inspection by the teacher or a practice teacher. They checked to see if our hair was combed, fingernails clean, and hands clean. Another ritual was singing "Good morning to you, good morning to you, we're all in our places with sun-shiny faces, oh this is the way to start a new day!"

The older pupils in the back of the room, sat on chunks of wood around the schoolhouse stove until the heat finally caught up with the cold parts of the room that had become frosty over night with no one there to put wood in the stove. We put our inkwells near the stove to thaw out so we could practice Palmer Method penmanship.

The seats we used at our desks were attached to the desk behind and folded up when not in use. Each grade went up front for "recitation" and sat in seats pulled down from the front of the front desks of each row. Recitation was when the teacher found out if the pupils were learning their lessons.

The toilets were partitioned off in the woodshed building. Boys had one end, girls the other. Believe me, we did not linger out there in winter. Our drinking water was in an earthen jug with a spigot. Fresh water was brought up from the nearest house every day by the biggest boy in school. We each had our own cups in our desks. One Christmas my Aunt Carrie had given me a silver collapsible cup in a leather case that I still have today.

Superintendent Martin Daniels visited school every so often to see how things were going and what we needed from his school supplies of paper, books, rulers and so on. I envied one girl who could do the "push and pull" and circle exercises for Palmer Method penmanship so smoothly. Mine looked rather uneven, and Mr. Daniels would sit beside me and help me practice. I never did get to be a good penman but my writing is readable.

From time to time we had a practice teacher from the Lyndon Normal School. Sometimes a class came from the normal school to "observe" for an hour or so.

It was exciting when the bookmobile made a visit bringing "new" books, exchanging them with the ones that had been brought before. We could get a book to read after all our work was done if it was still not time for us to be dismissed for the day.

We observed the holidays by making appropriate cut-outs

from colored construction paper after we had traced some patterns for Halloween, Thanksgiving, Christmas, Easter, Washington's and Lincoln's birthdays, Memorial, and other special days. We put on a Christmas program for our families. It was at night and the Christmas tree was sparkling and loaded with gifts and candy bags. After the program we would hear sleigh bells and Santa would come stomping and ho-hoing into the schoolroom with his red suit, boots, fat stomach and a bag full of presents.

We were like a family. If some of the bigger boys bullied some of the younger kids, there were always others would stick up for the younger ones. The teacher came out and played games with us. From my first grade through fourth Ida Lang Wheeler was my teacher and one evening each fall her husband would help her put on a corn roast for us.

Most of the time there were all eight grades in the school. If someone moved in or out of the neighborhood, it could change the number in a given grade, but that didn't happen very often. Most of us were farm families. Usually there were fifteen to twenty scholars in school each year. There were three of us in my grade through all eight years. Our schooling was as good as that in the village schools. We had the same textbooks and were prepared for Lyndon Institute as well as those from the bigger schools. Principal Ozias D. Mathewson liked to mention that from time to time.

A Civil War Veteran, Harvey S. Powers.

We Knew What Memorial Day Meant

T HE VETERANS MEMORIAL on Memorial Park near the railroad crossing in Lyndonville was dedicated on May 30, 1991, the year of Lyndon's bicentennial. It is a memorial to all veterans of Lyndon who served in any war.

One Civil War veteran lived here in Lyndonville for a long time. He was a widower named Harvey Powers. He lived at the home of his daughter.

Harvey S. Powers was a familiar figure in the Memorial Day parades. I was impressed to see this white-haired, white-bearded man riding in the parade. It helped me realize that history was real, not just in school books. Here was a living, breathing man who had actually fought in the Civil War.

Mr. Powers rode with his two hands—one on top of the other—resting on the head of a cane propped on the floor of the automobile. He wore his GAR (Grand Army of the Republic) uniform complete with hat.

Mr. Powers was born January 7, 1848, in Bath, N.H. He was 5 when his family moved to Barnet. He enlisted as a private from Barnet in Company A of the Ninth Vermont on September 9, 1864. He was in the battle at Chaplin Farm, the second battle at Fair Oaks and in the seige of Richmond. He came out of the war without a scratch and was mustered out as a private on June 13, 1865. After the war, he had a farm in Barnet, moved to Ryegate, and married Francena Carbee on June 22, 1868. They had a son, Frank, and a daughter, Alice.

In June 1934, Harvey Powers was chosen commander of the Vermont Grand Army of the Republic at the 67th national encampment at Montpelier. Six of the seven members of Chamberlin Post No. 1 (St. Johnsbury) attended the encampment. Mr. Powers was one of the members of this post.

The next meeting of the Chamberlin Post, the only one in Vermont still holding regular meetings, was really a reception in honor of newly elected Department Commander Powers. There were 50 people present to enjoy a dinner served by the Woman's Relief Corps and the Lucy A. Young Tent Daughters of the Veterans of the Civil War.

Even today, the Memorial Day parades bring back memories of Mr. Powers, the Civil War veteran, who gave meaning to what Memorial Day really meant. School children, even from the Lyndon one-room schools, carrying lilacs and flags for the cemetery, gathered in front of Music Hall (now the post office location), marching to the cemetery while the Lyndonville Military Band played the funeral march "Flee As A Bird." It was a solemn march meant to honor those war heroes. Coming back from the cemetery ceremonies, the band struck up livelier marches, but we as children, participating in this solemn occasion, knew what Memorial Day was all about and why we observed it.

Goblins, Ghouls and Ghosts

S CARY THINGS MAY BE LURKING around the dark corner, ready to pop out and scare the living heck out of you. Or maybe a black cat will run across your path, stop and snarl at you, his back arched and his tail puffed out to twice its normal size.

These are things that the older kids told the younger kids when Halloween approached. At our one-room Fletcher School, just up the road from the new Lyndon Town School, we went out for the afternoon recess, except the oldest girl, Madeline.

When we trooped back into the schoolroom, we stepped into a ghostly, scary cavern. All the shades were down and a leering jack-o-lantern lit by a flickering candle made the shadows in the room seem sinister. A moaning ghost and a cackling witch moved in and out around us. I think we older kids figured out that the witch was played by Madeline and the ghost by the teacher.

No one was really scared after that first moment of spooky surprise. Hadn't we been making black construction paper cats with arched backs and snarling jaws? And hadn't we been making orange pumpkins and putting this "art work" in the windows and across the top of the blackboard? And hearing ghost stories during reading time?

Of course we knew it was Halloween. But how did they get that washtub into the schoolroom and get it filled with

An old post card, postmarked 1922.

water and apples while we were on the playground without us seeing it!

We ducked for apples with our hands behind our backs, probably splashing the water around a bit. Did anyone try to push someone's head down? I hope not! Also, with our hands behind our backs, we tried to bite apples hanging from strings, but they kept bobbing against our faces. We played games and had some treats—candy, probably cookies, and punch.

We didn't go out trick or treating back in my school days era, at least nobody that I knew did, but we could have some of our friends in after school.

We older girls tried that trick where you pare a pippin (that's an apple, you know) around in a circle so the peeling from each was in one piece. We each slung a peeling around our heads three times, then let it (the peeling, you understand), drop to the floor behind us. It was supposed to form a letter—the initial of a boy friend. I think the peeling just laid there not doing anything. So I did not learn from the paring who I would pair with. (I must have flunked grammar that day)!

Another trick was to place an appleseed on each eyelid and name the appleseeds. The one that dropped from the eye first meant he is not so true as the other one. A blink could help make the decision.

We had another trick. With a lighted candle in one hand and a mirror in the other, we went down the dark cellar stairs to see the one who loved us in the mirror. (Perhaps the reason that didn't work was because we used flashlights.)

Today, many people have fun creating outdoor harvest figures with pumpkins, straw and old clothes, and painting faces on pumpkins. Lots of kids still make jack-o-lanterns by the old method, carving out the faces.

Did you say you were going trick-or-treating? Wait a minute—I'll get my broom and go with you.

THE LYNDON

GOLF CLUB

LYNDONVILLE, VERMONT

In the Shadow of Burke Mountain

SCORE CARD

"Pasturized" Golf

ALMOST 1,000 YEARS AGO, Romans, occupying parts of England and Scotland, played "paganica" in the open countryside with a bent stick and a "feathery"—a leather ball stuffed with feathers.

About 1457, a similar game called "golfe" and another popular game called "futeball" were banned by the parliament of King James II of Scotland because national defense was threatened by the neglect of archery. Who wanted to "shoote" an arrow when he could hit a ball with a "golfe sticke" or kick a ball with his "fute?" The ban was lifted after the peace treaty of 1502.

Some people around here still remember the old nine-hole golf links in the Fletcher pasture east of Lyndonville village, near enough for a player to get in a few holes after work.

Natural cropping of grass in a cow pasture made an ideal golf course. The obstacles and hazards were gullies, brooks, sand holes caused by erosion, trees and bushes, and cows, but there was a golf ball washer at almost every tee-off. Sometimes my father noticed a lump on a cow that had been hit by a golf ball. She probably didn't understand "Fore!"

The Lyndon golf course, originally known as the Abnaki Club, had been in operation since the late 1800s. It was reorganized and reactivated after World War I with a new constitution and bylaws, a renovated clubhouse, and the name

The Abnaki Clubhouse on golf links. Center front row, mother holding me, (c. 1922).

changed to Lyndon Golf Club. Several years later the clubhouse was taken down.

Pupils who carried the players' clubs were called "cadets" by Mary, Queen of Scots, and the word "caddy" or "caddie" came into use. According to the bylaws, caddies at the Lyndon course were to receive 15 cents for nine holes and 25 cents for 18 holes.

The number-one fairway was a bad place to slice a ball. If a player drove the ball over the fence, he was allowed to retrieve the ball and drive again, penalty one stroke. If the ball went over the fence again, he could retrieve it, place it one club length inside the fence and hit the ball from there, penalty one stroke. If he didn't go to the wooden barway to cross the barbed wire fence, he might find himself paying another penalty—a torn pair of pants.

Players seen beating around the bushes along the road by the first fairway were only looking for lost golf balls. Today the bushes are cut and on the number one fairway is a National Guard maintenance garage, Grappone Industrial, Inc., and VFW clubhouse.

The greenskeeper mowed the greens with a push-type non-motorized mower that he dragged up hill, down hill and across the brook from green to green. Then he would drag around a cylinder full of cement to roll the greens. Each green was fenced in to keep cows out.

The greenskeeper kept the golf ball washers filled with suds and the boxes at each tee-off pad filled with clay. Before golfers started using wooden or celluoid tees, at least around here, they teed-up for the drive by taking a handful of clay and forming a small mound on the clay tee-off pad.

Fairway number one was called "Speedwell." The next was "On Parade" and veered back near number one. From there the golfer played the third fairway, "Easy," to the green on the bank of a little brook that wandered aimlessly in a small valley. Number four, "Brightlook," took the player down the hill by cowpath, across the brook and on to the flat behind the Fletcher barns.

Across the flat was the fifth fairway, "Now or Never," and number six, "Beulah Land," brought the golfer back across the flat near the brook again. Number seven, "Brook Vale," was situated on another small flat back across the brook and if the player was lucky he could

PHOTO BY AUTHOR, 1940

Leona Hebert tees off.

get the ball across the brook but miss the big sand gully full of swallow holes on the left of the fairway.

The eighth green was located uphill on the "Matterhorn." The golfer could just see the top of the flag of the ninth green on the hilltop near the big elm tree. His drive had to be pretty accurate or the ball would go too much to the edge of the hill and roll down into sandy areas.

From the top of the hill, the ninth fairway was "Homeward Bound." If a player got a good drive from the top of the hill to the next one, his chances were good of rolling the ball onto the ninth green in the next stroke. This brought the player back full circle near tee number one and if he played another nine holes, he would have walked 4,222 yards—more than two and one half miles. Par for nine holes was 62 for men and 64 for women.

The fairways were named by ladies of the club to replace some of the names the men used that could be a little offensive to feminine ears in those days.

My brother and I and kids from Pinehurst hunted lost golf balls, put them through one of the washers and sold them to golfers for 10 or 15 cents. One in really good condition sometimes brought us 25 cents by a generous player.

The golf links was kept up for a while after World War II, in fact my mother dragged the mower around, mowed the greens and collected the green fees, but people were either too busy or went to fancier places to play. The course was abandoned by all except the cows.

For a long time though, there were some golfers who missed playing at the Fletcher links.

Let's Go Skating!

O N WINDSWEPT ICY PATCHES in fields and pastures, silvery skate blades flashed in the winter sun. A January thaw followed by cold snaps made many hollows into natural skating places. Sometimes after the freeze one could skate from one patch to another where little frozen rills connected them.

I was very small when I got double-runner skates one Christmas and tried them out on icy patches right on my own lawn. These skates did not stay attached to my shoes well and they skidded around on the ice. My parents soon realized that I was ready for the real thing—single runner skates—and got me a pair right away—the lace-up kind that stay on.

Through the years there were several places around Lyndonville where one could skate. One was the "cove" where the Passumpsic River backed up into the Darling field on Center Street. Way across the field the cove held quiet water—not part of the natural flowing river. We kids and grownups shoveled off the ice ourselves, built a bonfire for warmth and light—along with the moonlight—and skated for hours on crisp winter evenings.

Charles Darling, who lived in the house that is now the Guibord Funeral Home, owned the field. I believe it was the Village Improvement Society that had a hand in putting a rink here right next to Center Street and close to where the Ziter

PHOTO BY AUTHOR, 1940

Skating at the Center Street rink. Foreground, Sue Cornelius and George Ellsworth.

house is today. Walter (Pop) Andross, who lived nearby, kept a fire going in the warming shack, helped little children lace their skates, and jollied everybody. All the kids loved Pop. He had chocolate bars for sale—my favorite was a great big Baby Ruth bar that cost a nickel.

One rink was courtesy of the Charlands' Garage owned by George and Albert Charland. They provided the place between their garage (now Wheeler's sports store location) and the Jenne Garage with the winged horse Mobil sign (now Poulin's Feed location). A picture of that rink in my photo album is dated 1940.

I also remember a skating rink on the Lyndon Institute campus at some time or other, and there was a time when one was flooded on the Bandstand Park.

A rink was made by leveling snow into a hard-packed area. Boards were set up around the area, and the outer side packed with snow to make a rink fence. The rink was sprayed with water, probably from a nearby hydrant. After the recreational skaters left the ice, men or boys played hockey. The rink was sprayed again each night to make the ice smooth after the hours of exuberant use.

Snap-the-Whip indulged in by some could be exciting, particularly for the one on the end who really got a thrill when everyone let go of hands. Couples skated with hands crossed, in rhythmic grace. Some of us admired those who showed off their figure eights or cut corners in either direction. As for me, I could cut corners easily in one direction only—counter clockwise. Skating backwards was fun too, especially the thrill of hitting an unseen bad spot in the ice that sent you flying unexpectedly through space.

A good part of my leisure hours from childhood on up were spent at the skating rink—whichever one was in operation. Even when visiting my Aunt Carrie in St. Johnsbury I skated on the Portland Street or the Winter Street rink.

"It is a Queer Winter in These Parts"

ON DECEMBER 21, 1866, the Lyndon weekly newspaper, the *Vermont Union*, reported five inches of snow and that the first sleighs of the season were out. A week later, December 28, the paper said, "We do not know whether to call this winter or not. We have had one day of poor sleighing and one cold snap—last Friday morning the thermometer stood at 20 degrees below zero and the ground was just covered with snow enough to make the appearance of sleighing. This was followed by rain and regular April weather. This morning we had a freeze but no appearance of snow. It is a queer winter in these parts."

Earlier that fall, October 5, the paper reported that it was "almost July weather and makes a fine contrast after having so much cold and wet." On November 2, three inches of snow was reported; then on November 16, "Everybody sat up Tuesday night but no one saw a shower, though a few meteors were seen. The phenomenon might have occurred during the day and therefore invisible." Evidently, it was the time of a meteor shower, but there was no suggestion that the phenomenon might be the cause for the "queer" weather.

Weather is a popular topic of conversation, probably because weather is something eveyone experiences. Mark Twain said, "One of the brightest gems in New England weather is the dazzling uncertainty of it." With the sophisticated weather

The Winter Sports
Seated: Anna Kerr, Maude Robinson, Kate Cable with dog (name not known). Standing: a Mrs. Burns, Eva Wilkie, Emma Fletcher (my mother), Hermine Cusson, Annie Shonyo. My mother crocheted her hat, including the flowers on it.

instruments of today it is not quite so uncertain, though old timers could often tell by the looks of things what was coming because they had had a lifetime of noticing weather signs.

January thaws were normal occurrences and most of the time there was enough snow on the ground so that even though it rained and warmed up a few days it didn't take away all the snow. It would freeze and we would have a few days of sliding on crust before the next snow storms came.

In one of my albums are photos dated January 17, 1932. The ground is absolutely bare, not even a tiny drift of snow left anywhere. My father did not remember seeing ground completely bare in January before. He and I took pictures of what he thought we might never see again—absolute bare ground in January.

When we had the usual January thaws and freeze up after, it made a wonderful crust for sliding. We could go on our sleds all the way across a big field even if there was only a little slope to it. We could slide on steeper slopes in an old dishpan, or on cardboard. We could race and run on the icy crust.

Then it would snow and if we tried to walk in the field, we would be almost up to our waists when our feet broke all the way down through the crust that the new snow had softened.

Snowshoeing was my mother's favorite outdoor pastime. Her stride on snowshoes was wonderful to behold. Snowshoe club members took turns hosting the hot cocoa and sandwiches after an evening on snowshoes in the winter moonlight. One crisp winter evening, restaurant owner Fred Shonyo had delicious corn chowder ready for his wife and her snowshoe party when they came back and it was a highlight of the season.

One day my mother and I snowshoed over a snow bridge on a brook. My mother broke through, but not down into the water. She slid over backward trying to get her snowshoes up the bank. We were laughing so hard we had difficulty getting one of her snowshoes off so she could get a foothold to climb out.

Skiing was a little different in those days and cost nothing to use. We kids put our feet in the ski straps and held them on with jar rubbers or rings cut from old inner tubes. The first ride down the hill broke a trail. By skiing down the same track over and over we could go a little farther and a little faster each time. Sometimes, for a change, we would put our skis together and sit on them, holding onto the straps and ride in that way. We rode the scooter or jumper my father made, using a barrel stave for a runner. My mother was better than us kids in balancing that and could go all the way down the hill without tipping over.

Some of the kids from the Ville would come up to our pasture with a toboggan. Some of the bigger boys had a traverse, a big plank on two sleds. A traverse went best on the packed roads and was steered by the front sled. There have been some wild spills with traverses out of control on icy roads. Everybody got up, brushed themselves off and were ready to go again.

After a January thaw, we could often skate for a while where puddles in the hollow spots froze, but usually we went to the rink at Lyndonville.

Of course we did all the other winter things kids do. It was fun on Saturdays when the neighborhood kids could get together. We made angels in the snow, played fox and geese, threw snowballs, rolled in the snow and built snowmen. When we were done, we swept each other off with the shed broom before going into the house. How many people remember the smell of wet wool socks drying by the wood fired kitchen stove? It wasn't exactly unpleasant—it was just noticeable!

Birds eye view of Lyndonville, Vt.

Village Life

...oto before 1924. Half of Depot Street burned in 1924, including the large
...ite buildings, left center.

My Home Town-Before My Time

I N 1788 DANIEL CAHOON began cutting trees and built his log cabin in Lyndon. He began his clearing not far from the Big Falls on the Passumpsic River. Apparently the lure of "new" unworked land made hardships and loneliness bearable.

There is a story that Daniel, while crossing the Passumpsic River, had the misfortune to drop his axe. Repeated dives into the cold water failed to retrieve it. This meant a long walk to Newbury thirty miles away to get another. Newbury was already an "old" town, having been settled in 1760.

By 1790 there were 59 people including 20 women living in Lyndon. The first town meeting was held July 4, 1791, the same year (March 4, 1791) that Vermont became the fourteenth state of the union after being an independent republic for fourteen years.

It has been said that Lyndon was named for Josiah Lyndon Arnold, son of one of the proprietors. It was also said that Lyndon was named after the governor of Rhode Island. Perhaps both could be right because Jonathan Arnold apparently named his son after the Rhode Island governor, Josiah Lyndon.

Until 1866, there was no village where Lyndonville is now. If anyone wanted a lawyer, a newspaper, a hotel room, a drink at a tavern, a doctor, a preacher, attend church, go to an academy, mail a letter, banking services, buy a carriage, or much of anything else, he went to Lyndon Corner, or Lyndon Center.

Scene in Early Lyndonville

In 1809 four denominations, Baptists, Congregationalists, Methodists, and Universalists built the union meeting house at Lyndon Center. The town paid a portion of the cost of the building to share it for public meetings. Long after these denominations built their own separate churches the town still used the old meeting house for public meetings and voting. It was also used for other community events. It is still known as the Town House and is the oldest public building remaining in town.

Once the mills were established people moving into town built their settling houses, the required 18 feet square feet (at least) on the floor, and tilled the required five acres to prove their good faith as settlers rather than as speculators. For a time the log cabins remained as homes for newcomers, until they too, could build their own cabin or house. Today log cabins on the Vermont landscape are mostly built by "people from away" who enjoy the rustic look on the green hills and in the woods, but settlers built log cabins as an expediency and could not wait to get their comfortable frame houses built.

These original houses were low-ceilinged, usually a story and a half, with kitchen/family room on the ground floor and a sleeping chamber above. Later, higher posted 2½ story houses were sometimes added, often with two rooms each side of a main hall both upstairs and down, with the third floor an attic area for storage of family relics. Some people built 1½ story farmhouses. Many village houses were large, built by the lawyers, physicians, and businessmen men. Later, for a while, most new houses were one-floor with finished rooms in the basement. Now two-story houses are in again and we see many new ones.

The railroad came to Lyndon and north to Newport by 1857. In 1866 the company, the Connecticut and Passumpsic Rivers Railroad bought more than 300 acres of land in Lyndon after their shops burned down in St. Johnsbury. It was not long before a new village flourished near the railroad shops and depot. This became Lyndonville officially when the post office was established on April 13, 1868.

When the railroad company started selling lots there were

restrictions to prevent the new village from becoming a shack town like many places that grew too fast. For example, my great uncle, William Fletcher paid the railroad company $350 for a corner lot. The deed stated that he was not to build any nearer than 20 feet to either Center Street or West Street (now Park Avenue), and he was not to build anything less than two stories high. When he moved to California in 1885, he sold the property to the Folsoms who had the house moved to a lot on Park Avenue and they built a new house on the corner lot.

Before there was a village of Lyndonville, communities grew in Lyndon's outlying districts, such as East Lyndon, Red Village, Mt. Hunger, Pudding Hill, Squabble Hollow, Mosquito District, Cold Hill, and others, each with its own one-room school. There were three village graded schools at Lyndonville, Lyndon Center, and Lyndon Corner respectively. East Lyndon even had its own church (Methodist).

The railroad opened up a whole new world. Special trains ran at special rates for special events—fairs, Fourth of July celebrations, a visiting dignitary, a minstrel show, a concert, or a ball, and brought entertainers and speakers who performed in the village (Lyndonville) hall.

People in the villages generally had a garden, kept a family cow, a few hens for eggs, occasionally one fattened for Sunday dinner (dinner was midday even in the village), perhaps a pig (great garbage disposal), and a horse or two for driving if they were affluent enough.

Many a carriage barn became the garage of today. Some country homes (outside the villages) were small family farms; a few farmers peddled milk to villagers who did not keep a cow. Farms sustained the family, but the father might be a mill worker or a carpenter for cash money. Eggs and butter were traded for groceries at the local grocery store, or the farmer's wife had the egg money to use since it was usually she who tended the hens. Many farmers turned to dairying when the Lyndonville Creamery was built in 1890 and milk could be shipped to Boston by train.

"Clear Running Water"

THE PASSUMPSIC RIVER runs through the town of Lyndon, separating Lyndonville and Lyndon Center, but the white man's discovery of it is told in the history of St. Johnsbury written by Edward T. Fairbanks in 1912.

Many years ago Algonquin Indians traveled a river they called Poosumpsuk, meaning "clear running water." In 1755 Stephen Nash was commissioned by the British army to head north into the wilderness to determine if the Indians might be a threat to the Massachusetts Colony.

Nash explored the Passumpsic, camping where the Moose River met the Passumpsic (in what became St. Johnsbury). He wrote in his journal that he saw no signs of "the enimy" but saw one moose. "The uplands of the Passumsuk are stony and hard and not good for settlements, but I saw small pieces of meadow by the river and a goodly number of falls and rapids."

When white men decided that lands along the Passumpsic looked promising for settlements, an advertisement appeared in the Providence Gazette of June 27, 1787. It said, "New lands on or near the pleasant and healthful River Passumpsick . . . Titles to every lot will be had from the original grantees, payment to be made in cattle, country produce and labour . . . [signed] Jonathan Arnold." Arnold was one of the 64 proprietors of the Providence Plantation that became Lyndon. Jonathan

PHOTO COURTESY KEN BARBER'S PETERSON COLLECTION

The Passumpsic River. The Little Falls and the Vail electric plant (April 16, 1916).

Arnold, Daniel Cahoon and Daniel Owen was the committee that had set the lines of the town in 1781.

No matter how the name of the river had been spelled it came to be accepted as "Passumpsic." At the heighth of land in Brighton, Essex County, springs and small feeder brooks trickling and seeping southward down this wooded mountainside give rise in Newark to the Passumpsic. It meanders leisurely across flat meadows in East Newark and is joined by brooks, including Mill brook which comes tumbling off East Mountain and trips head over heels into the Passumpsic on Route 114.

The West Branch begins in Westmore on the southern slopes of Mt. Pisgah at Lake Willoughby and coming through Burke meets the East Branch north of Lyndonville near Folsom's Crossing. The river is fed by numerous streams all the way to Barnet, about 34 miles in all where it ends and flows into the Connecticut River at Round Island just below Fifteen Mile Falls.

"The railway is obliged to cross it [the Passumpsic] about 30 times in 25 miles, and in one section of 7 miles there are 11 bridges," observed the *Vermont Union* of Sept. 18, 1868. The leisurely pace through low meadowlands causes the stream to wind and twist, almost back on itself at times. It has been referred to as a liquid corkscrew.

The river had its swimming holes and its skating "rinks." Before the swimming pool was built in Powers Park, an instructor conducted swimming lessons in the river near the Miller's Run covered bridge at Lyndon Center. Skaters took advantage of the cove near the river on Charles Darling's meadow (Center Street) where the river backed up, and froze into a smooth skating "rink." Nowadays a favorite sport on the Passumpsic in Lyndon is the annual April canoe race.

Sometimes the river goes on rampages, causing floods— the worst one in 1927.

Even as late as 1981, a 3.5 mile canoe trip beginning at the bridge by Lynburke Motel and ending by what is now Day's Inn afforded a chance to see some green herons (we weren't lucky enough to see a blue heron that day). When some crows put up a holler we saw an owl suddenly desert his roost and his daytime nap as the crows chased him out of a tall tree.

There were a few fallen trees and some rubbish. There was a chassis or two of some very old cars. A boy was fishing from the Lyndon Center bridge as we came along. "What are you catching?" we called up to him. "Dace," he answered, pulling one in. Trout had been abundant in the Passumpsic, but later, with dams, mill refuse and sewage polluting the waters, one is more apt to find suckers and dace. Now a sewage plant keeps the river cleaner and the Lyndonville Rotary Club and Lyndon State College students have done a lot to clean rubbish out of the river.

The Passumpsic meanders and winds through meadowlands, but there are enough rapids and falls here and there so that mills have flourished along its length. The Great Falls and Little Falls in Lyndon, former mill sites, now produce some of the electricity for the Lyndonville Electric Department.

Swinging Over the Passumpsic

I N A DAY WHEN most people walked to work, the line of least resistance was important for saving time. To save many steps, probably as much as a mile, a swing footbridge spanned the Passumpsic River from the big field at Lyndon Center to Powers Park where workmen could come out at Grove Street and head across the street directly to the railroad shops.

Sometimes other people used this swaying footbridge as well. A lady from Chautauqua took a group of us youngsters on a nature walk once which included a forced march across this bridge. At least for me it was forced—not by her—by me.

Climbing to the top of an apple or maple tree, or climbing 30 feet up to the top of the barn to jump in the hay held no fears for me, but that bridge was a different matter. It scared the living daylights out of me. It really did swing and sway, but not with Sammy Kaye.

In the first place, this narrow little bridge was high above the river and I could not swim then. In the second place there was one cable for a hand rail on one side only, and in the third place, when some of the braver kids realized there was a scaredy cat on it, they ran across or jumped up and down to make it really swing. In the meantime some of us were inching along, half inch by half inch, hanging on for dear life, both hands on that cable.

The swing bridge between Lyndon Center and Powers Park, Lyndonville. Horace Locklin and Charles Parker, c. 1904.

The bridge I remember, a later one than the photo with this story, was high above the water so that when the ice moved out in the spring, it would not be so apt to damage the bridge. It had to be repaired, however, sometimes even rebuilt in the spring. In winter, a path was kept across the field when possible and workers crossed on the ice. Some of us attending Lyndon Institute, our high school, took a short cut across the ice from behind the Lyndonville Graded School, coming out behind the "Matty House" (Mathewson House, the girls' dorm). It was a long, cold walk across the big field on 20 or 30 degrees below zero days especially if the wind blew. But then, it was a long cold walk around the road to the Center, too, and crossing the ice was quicker. When the ice was bare, it was much quicker yet!

The approach to the swing bridge was nine steps up (at least for the later bridge). Mary Hubbard Parker definitely remembers nine steps. Her father, Clayton Hubbard, was one of the workers who constructed the later bridge or repaired it in the spring. She remembers as I do that short planks were laid across the two supporting under cables—not lengthwise as in the photo of the earlier bridge.

Clayton Hubbard died in December 1941; the bridge went out with the ice in the spring of 1942, as Mary remembers, and was never rebuilt.

The old swing bridge is no longer needed. Now almost everyone drives to work (not to the railroad shops, they are long gone) and can swing through Lyndon Center and wheel across the concrete bridge on Route 122 to Lyndonville.

The Passumpsic Runneth Over

ON THAT FRIDAY, November 3, 1927, when we walked home from our one-room school it was pouring rain. It had rained for days. The ground was saturated. Normal October rainfall was 2.48 inches, but in 1927 it was 5.64 inches.

On Saturday morning up here on the hill we didn't know anything about a flood. My father loaded his evening and morning's milk into his pickup and went to the creamery. Except he didn't get to the creamery.

After a while he came back and said to my mother, "Emma, take the kids and go down street. You'll see something you've never seen before." He put the milk cans back into the cold water tub, and went to do his barn chores, while my mother, and Gordon and I took the pickup and drove down street.

We could go as far as the railroad crossing on Broad Street, as far as the end of Main Street, both southward. Heading north on Main Street, we could go almost to the filling station. There was no getting to the creamery on the other side of the river which had become a torrent rushing across meadow and streets.

We watched while creamery men went around in boats to see what could be done about the pigs in the piggery and the horses in some stalls on the property. Finally, someone decided to open the pens and let the pigs loose to let them swim to

The Road to Lyndon Corner

safety, but pigs with their short legs often cut their own throats with their toenails and I don't remember if any survived.

The water was up to the horses' necks in the barn, so they were turned loose also. One or two, I remember, made it to the street and someone threw blankets over them and ran them up and down the street to get them warmed up. I don't know what the farmers did with their milk until things were in operation again.

After a while we drove to the south end of Main Street. One man laid a brick on the edge of the water in front of Charlie Darling's house (now Guibord's Funeral Home) to judge if, or how fast the water was receding. Next door to Darling's, Jim Dexter's hens had taken refuge on the roosts and some dropped their eggs into the water.

The next day, Dad took me with him to see what we could of the damage the flood had done. I particularly remember driving up the East Burke road, but before we got to Mt. Hunger the road ended. The river had taken over.

PHOTO BY ALEX MCLANE

The Road to Lyndon Center.
The spot in the water toward the left is a hack (taxi) that was overtaken by the flood and had to be abandoned.

Later that day my mother took Gordon and me with her to go to Lyndon Center to see how her friend Bertha Greenwood had fared. The piano was ruined, but the wooden bedsteads had floated up to the ceiling and were undamaged. When the Greenwoods had first entered the house after the water had receded somewhat, they looked into the basement and saw an agate pan with eggs floating around on the moving water. When the water went down, the pan of eggs set back down on the table where it had been placed before the flood. It took hoes and shovels to remove the foul-smelling silt and mud from the floors in the house.

Electric and telephone poles and wires were down everywhere. Many bridges were impassable, railroad tracks were twisted and roads were washed out. They were mostly unpaved then, even from Lyndonville to St. Johnsbury. My mother and

Gordon and I got royally stuck on the road that goes from Route 5 to Lyndon Center. A big truck came along and pulled us out. But of course like everyone else, we were curious to see the sights.

Everyone went to work to restore and recover Vermont and Governor John Weeks sent an urgent appeal to Washington. This was when Honorable Herbert Hoover, President Calvin Coolidge's Secretary of Commerce, came to Vermont to study the conditions. It was his first visit, and he was told that he would see "Vermont at its worst." After a week in Vermont his comment was, "I have seen Vermont at its worst, but I have seen Vermonters at their best."

A Belfry Bell, Stained Glass, and a Pipe Organ

THE SOUND OF THE BELL in the steeple of the First Congregational Church in Lyndonville still lingers in my mind. When I entered the vestry for Sunday School it was impressive to me to see the sexton pull on the thick rope that rang the bell in the steeple. When the bell turned back up so did the rope. His hands, gripping the rope, were as high as he could reach. He was almost—but not quite—lifted off his feet.

During the fire in 1967, the bell was pulled down to the ground before it could fall on firefighters. The impact cracked the bell. It might have been recast for the new church but in this day and age of wonderful technology the cost would have been prohibitive. Lawrence Cassady and his son Gary built a covered support for the bell on the lawn by the new church, and planted flowers at the base in memory of Gary's mother, Margaret Cassady. The bell is also a mute reminder of the old Gothic-style church that served its people for 95 years.

In 1872 when the original church was under construction, a subscription paper was started to raise $400 for a bell. The pastor's wife, Mrs. Perrin B. Fisk, promised the next wedding fee toward the bell. Traditionally ministers gave their wives the wedding fees for their own use. The fine sounding bell, keyed in B flat, arrived in July 1872, in time to be hung during the construction of the church.

First Congregational Church, Lyndonville, Vermont, c. 1952.

The curved top area of the tall windows in the sanctuary had stained glass pictures. One was a dove with an olive branch, one was a lamb, one was an open Bible. There were others, eight in all. The stained glass gleamed in the morning light.

The raised choir loft was located each side of the marvelous pipe organ. A hot air register in the middle aisle could cause a little consternation when it lifted ladies dresses, as they stepped over it just as the heat blew on. One time when the choir was processing down the aisle, a member caught her high heel in the register and had to wriggle her foot out of her shoe in order to continue.

When the Sunday school children put on the Christmas program, the tree reached to the top of the high ceiling. Wrapped gifts and candy boxes hung from the tree that gleamed with tinsel rope, ornaments, and real candles. That was pretty impressive to a child.

As we grew older, we joined the Christian Endeavor, the youth group of the time. The girls waited on tables at the church suppers. Some of the young people then taught Sunday School, sang in the senior choir, and some even joined the church.

The church was built in 1871 and 72 after the Society was formed in 1870. My great uncle and aunt, William H. and Emma (Brown) Fletcher of Lyndonville, were charter members. My great grandparents Joseph and Ruth (Elliott) Fletcher and family had come to the farm here in 1839 before there was a Lyndonville, so they went to the Lyndon Corner Congregational Church.

After the fire in 1967 the church was replaced by a new one on the same foundation.

One Hundred Years Old and Still Ticking

ONCE A WEEK for three generations someone in the Aubin family picks up the large crank and winds the "town" clock. It has been stopped for repairs only for short periods, and for a longer period when the clock face and hands were thoroughly redone with modern weatherproof material a few years ago.

Around 1893, the progress of raising funds for a village clock was reported faithfully in the *Vermont Union*. It took almost two years to raise the money. The Catholic church, a wooden one, St. Martin's, had burned down in 1892. It was replaced by the brick Romanesque-style St. Elizabeth's with a steeple designed to house the clock. The Village Improvement Society had a lot to do with raising funds for the clock, including Friday night dances in the Village (Music) Hall.

In May the *Union* reported, "About ten more feet remains to be put on the steeple. The building is bound to show off finely when completed." By November the 2,000 pound bell was raised to the steeple. The bell belongs to the Catholic church.

Railroad ties were laid down beside the church, the bell put on them, then a line of men holding a long rope, pulled the bell up, more ties were put on the pile, the bell pulled up to those, more ties placed, and in this manner the bell was finally swung into the tower.

PHOTO BY AUTHOR, 1994

Clock in the St. Elizabeth Church steeple.

Then in October the *Union* said, "The town clock fund is raised and the clock bought, we hear, and why is not the clock in position to announce the time?" A delay occurred, it was said, because some subscribers to the fund seemed to have reservations about having the clock in that steeple. There was a little talk of putting a steeple on the Village Hall (Music Hall) and placing the clock there. The Catholic people said that if the clock was placed in their steeple it must always remain there as the steeple was designed and built for such a clock.

When the clock arrived there seemed to be no trouble with signing an agreement between the village trustees and Father Joseph Paquet who signed on behalf of the Catholic church. It was agreed the Catholics would manage the clock while the village would maintain it. Though the agreement was made with the village of Lyndonville, it is usually called the "town clock."

The clock finally purchased was a better one than at first planned for, which may have been partly the reason for delay in getting it. According to Village Improvement Society records and the newspaper, it was due in large part, to the efforts of Mrs. Harley E. Folsom, president of the newly organized V.I.S., village trustee Austin W. Houghton, and to Theodore N. Vail, who gave a generous subscription to make up all deficiencies so as to obtain a much better clock than first intended.

At last the *Vermont Union* editor was satisfied. This report appeared in the November 9, 1894 issue: "After a long struggle the $600 clock was placed in the Catholic steeple and struck the hours of time on Friday."

The clock on its four heavy iron legs bears a plate with the inscription, "Seth Thomas, Thomaston, Conn., Oct. 18, 1894." The main clock works is on one level in the steeple, the shaft and cables running up through another level to operate the four sets of hands. When the clock needed work done, Paul Aubin repaired it. He had to climb to the very top to do certain repairs.

The heavy metal pendulum hanging just under the floor on which the main clock works rests, ticks back and forth faithfully.

An immense metal weight drops with each strike of the hour or half hour, causing a hammer to strike the big bell to sound the time. When pulled up—by a washing machine motor devised by Gerald Aubin to save pulling it up manually—the weight is up in the level beside the works, but at the end of the week after striking all those hours, it is in the basement, almost 60 feet down from its highest position.

There have been times when something stuck and the bell did not sound the hours for a time, but the hands kept right on doing their job. When the bell is rung for other reasons, such as for services, it is done by the rope that makes the bell swing against the clapper inside it.

The *Union* reported on Nov. 16, 1894, "The dials show well from any part of the village and the tap on the big bell is heard, with favorable wind, miles away." Not everybody had watches in those days, but even today it is a habit with some of us to glance up at the big clock on the hill to note the time when doing errands and keeping appointments within many areas of the village and town. The four dials are well-lit at night.

Dummies

THE STOP SIGN BARRELS which were placed on Depot Street in 1992 to remind drivers to stop and wait their turn, are reminders of the street dummies with the signs that said, "Keep to the right." That's right, they were called dummies—but they kept motorists on their own side of the street. They were also known as "silent policemen."

There were four along Depot Street, one at the intersection of Main Street, one at Elm Street, one at Church Street, and one at Broad Street.

An earlier photo shows the dummy at Depot and Broad streets located just at the entry to Broad Street. Apparently, after the 1924 fire, it was moved more onto Depot Street to take care of traffic going east and west, as well as turning onto or from Broad Street. It was where the second barrel from the railroad track is now. That dummy could also have been moved for easier access into the Corner Garage from either Broad or Depot streets. The Corner Garage building on the corner took the place of the Stern Block that burned down in the fire.

In this photo and the earlier picture mentioned, the lower two globes were white and the top globe was red. The later pictures—probably around the late thirties—show that all these globes on each dummy were white. Perhaps the white globes were less expensive if they had to be replaced, and since traffic

DEPOT STREET, LYNDONVILLE, VERMONT

Traffic "dummy" or "silent policeman." The building on the left was the "Old Corner Boarding House," torn down in the 1950s to make way for the Plaza Theater, now the White Market.

did not have to stop in certain directions it was probably better to discontinue the globe that glowed red when turned on.

The increase in traffic, the use of trucks in place of railroads, and the escalated speed of traffic made it necessary to remove the dummies sometime around the early fifties.

Splashing Fountains

T HE SPLASHING FOUNTAIN in the park in the center of Lyndonville, now called Bandstand Park, helps set a summer scene that has been enjoyed by the community for many years, though the fountain of today is not the same fountain of earlier days.

On Sept. 3, 1880, the *Vermont Union* stated: "A fine iron fountain, eleven feet high, has been selected for the center of the park. The piece is surmounted by a female figure and a swan from whose mouth a stream of water will be thrown up to fall back into a dripping pan and thence into a second and larger pan and thence to a cement reservoir 16 feet in diameter. When completed with trees, walks and fountain, the park will be a great attraction for the village." Part of this is also quoted in the history book, *Lyndon, Gem In the Green*, begun by Dr. Venila Shores some years ago and completed in 1986 by Ruth McCarty.

The iron "pans" or basins, were ornate. In a time when nudity was reserved for the privacy of one's own home, the female figure with her hand on the swan, was molded with draped garments appearing to billow gently around her as though blown by a soft breeze. This represented a cooling effect on a hot day, along with the flowing water and shade of tall stately elm trees.

On June 12, 1885, the *Union* said, "The fountain on the park has received a coat of paint and the woman on the top

Park, Lyndonville. Vt.

The Lady and the Swan, in village park.

has been bronzed, making her look much more fascinating than before." Evidently the lady was not considered "fascinating" enough to keep after some years, although the reason given for her removal was that it was thought to be too heavy for the fountain.

The fountain itself was taken out in 1952 to cut down on maintenance work by village employees, so it was said. Another "hearsay" is that it was sold for scrap. The packed earth walks from each corner and from each side of the park to the fountain were eliminated. Elm trees died and were cut down.

For about twenty years there was no fountain and no water in the concrete basin left after the removal of the fountain. During a few years prior to the 1976 (U.S.) and the 1977 (Vermont as an independent state) bicentennials, a Fountain Restoration Committee was formed to raise funds and place another fountain on the park.

One of similar size was out of reach financially, but the committee did find one that could be purchased with the $2,000

*The fountain in Railroad Park. Post card sent by my father,
Earl H. Fletcher, to Frank McGinnis, 1909, given to me by
McGinnis' daughter, Margaret McGinnis Kerr.*

fountain restoration funds. The committee also raised another
$1,000 for maintenance.

Water for the fountain in 1880 was furnished at first by the
Lyndonville Water Company, a corporation owned by Robert
Pettigrew, J.W. Copeland, Jeremy Pearl, and I.W. Sanborn. The
fountain of today takes little water because of the use of a recycling pump.

Though the fountain obtained by the Restoration Committee is smaller, it helped allay the feeling that something was
missing in the park for so many years.

Though they are not the regal elms of yesterday a variety
of other trees have been planted as well as shrubs and flowers
through the efforts of the Lyndon Woman's Club. The Victorian
lamp post with the globed lights that the Village Improvement
Society placed in the park in 1913 were taken up, restored and
put back in the park in time for Lyndon's bicentennial in 1991.

In 1885 $500 was raised by subscription for a fountain on what was then Depot Park near the railroad tracks. This was a smaller fountain with a cupid-like figure holding up something from which water sprayed and ran down into an iron basin, then into the concrete pool. Along with flower beds and trees, this park provided a fine welcome to visitors who alighted from the train. This fountain was taken out many years ago.

Merry Cyclers Trough

SERVICE STATIONS are everywhere for refueling "horse-less carriages." In the "old days," a "service station" for a horse might be a watering trough. A refreshing drink of water could go a long way in getting good mileage out of a horse.

Railroad Park on Broad Street still has one of these old-time watering troughs. A few people have asked about this trough when walking onto the park for a closer look at the Veterans Memorial which was dedicated on Memorial Day, May 20, 1991. The park which has been called Depot Park or Railroad Park is now renamed appropriately, Memorial Park.

During work day hours the trough is hardly noticeable because cars park in front of it, but it has been there for more than 90 years. On the side of the trough toward the park it says, "Presented by the Merry Cyclers." The side toward the street is inscribed with the date "1898."

"The Merry Cyclers" was an operetta sponsored by the Lyndonville Village Improvement Society. The proceeds were to be used to replace an old wooden tub with a village water trough of granite. The 60 performers, all "homefolk," rehearsed for two months under the direction of Homer Wilson, who was for many years the director of the Lyndonville Military Band. The Merry Cyclers was a 2½ hour entertainment of comedy and music. It was held two evenings in Music Hall and netted

Merry Cyclers Trough.

the Village Improvement Society $250, more than enough to obtain the trough at a cost of $200.

Later that summer the trough was installed. It was "hewn" of granite, shaped like a log setting on two granite tree "stumps." The trough was the right height so the horse could easily drink without unchecking. Even the dogs weren't forgotten. On the outer ends at the bottom of each stump was a drinking "cup" for their convenience. Curbing placed along the park kept horses from treading on the grass.

This park, now called Memorial Park, for a long time had a two-tier fountain with a figure on top, and a bandstand, but after the park on Main Street was developed to its full extent, the bandstand was moved to that park at some time. It seems that some people thought that it might be rather dangerous for children to be running around at a band concert so near the railroad. The fountain there was also removed. I don't remember either the fountain or the bandstand on that park.

The park is serving the public well with the new Veterans Memorial dedicated to service people from the entire town of Lyndon, the information booth for travelers' directions, benches for sitting, and an ice cream stand nearby. And though it has been many years since water filled the unique trough, it now can, and sometimes does, serve as an excellent flower planter.

Lion of the Republic in Lyndonville

I T WAS 8 A.M. the morning of November 27, 1894 when Luther B. Harris, cashier of the Lyndonville National Bank viewed the vault that stood in the midst of burning coals.

He refused to be discouraged, though earlier that morning a raging fire had swept through Depot Street, destroying 23 buildings, burning out 28 families and 30 of the 34 business places including the Ide Block where the bank was housed in one of the rooms. The block had been built by my great uncle, William H. Fletcher. When he moved to California in 1885 he sold it to George Ide.

"We are all right," Harris said, "and will soon be doing business at the old express office." The ruins were still smoldering when the directors held a meeting instructing the cashier to notify real estate owners that the bank would lend all the money needed to rebuild, making conditions "as easy as safety of funds would permit."

They arranged to build a temporary shelter and began making plans for a permanent fireproof building of their own, "to be located and designed to beautify the village."

Having saved their papers and stationery, with $1,000 insurance, and the confidence of the people, the bank was soon doing a lively business. By the spring and summer 1895, new blocks began to rise, replacing the temporary shacks hastily constructed for winter.

One of two lions at the Lyndonville Savings Bank and Trust Company.

Lyndonville Bank, many years before remodeling. The lions stood prominently on high pedestals.

The new bank, located on Broad Street, was a handsomely designed two-story structure of brick. It was an impressive building and it looked like a bank. The interior was handsome quartered oak paneling throughout with wrought iron grille work from counters to ceiling between the public and the tellers.

While in Florence, Italy some years later, Luther Harris was impressed by Donatello's "Il Marzocco," or "Lion of the

Republic" that had been placed in the Ringeria of the Palazzo Vecchio even before the discovery of America.

Donatello was Donato di Nicola Bardi, a famous sculptor of the Renaissance. His magnificent lion with the fleur-de-lis shield has been regarded as the most beautiful animal statue in the world.

Through the influence of three American artists, Harris arranged to have replicas cast in bronze and shipped to America to "enhance the town and enjoyment of the people" of Lyndonville as a reward for their confidence and friendly relations to the bank.

In a letter to Harris from Florence dated January 23, 1905, Larkin Mead, the American sculptor said, "I have received your check for 1800 lire which is for payment of the two Donatello Lions cast for you in bronze by Fonderia Galli.

"I have seen the bronze casts and they have done them magnificently. Your town is very fortunate in possessing them. They will be great educators and will create a taste for the beautiful."

The lion statues arrived in May 1905, by way of the Straits of Gibraltar, across the ocean, then over land by rail until they reached Lyndonville where they were placed on granite pedestals at each side of the bank steps. In 1922 the Lyndonville Savings Bank and the Lyndon National Bank together became the Lyndonville Savings Bank and Trust Company, but the lions remained on their prominent pedestals until the bank was completely rebuilt in 1962 and the fortress-style bank was lost forever.

Some area townspeople became concerned when the lions disappeared from their vigil, but they were safe in some remote area of the construction while the bank employees kept on working under the rebuilding conditions.

The famous lions, with all the appearance of benevolent protectors, now posing on pedestals of black granite from the Andes of South America, once again took up their watch over the village of Lyndonville, but from a far less prominent position.

Some children have found the lions appealing. While the lions were sitting on the ground in 1905 waiting to be placed on their pedestals, a little girl walked up to them and offered them a bite of her cookie. Many years later when my granddaughter Mary was a toddler, she would have me lift her up so she could hug each one in turn.

Darling Inn, A Gem in the Green

O N JANUARY 21, 1924 a fire devastated a large portion of the business district of Lyndonville, including the hotel then called Lyndon Hotel. Subscriptions were collected for a new hotel and in 1927 a meeting of the subscribers was held with directors E.A. Darling, O.D. Mathewson, H.E. Folsom, John L. Norris, D.I. Grapes, and W.E. Riley, all prominent businessmen.

Elmer A. Darling, a Burke native, was chosen to head the enterprise. His long experience in the Fifth Avenue Hotel in New York City enabled him to contribute his finesse and expertise to the appointments of one of the finest hotels in the northeast, the Darling Inn. He saw to it only the best materials were used in the construction. He requested, and was given the privilege of personally furnishing the dining room.

The new hotel was named for Darling, though not by his request. His friends thought it a fitting gesture since he was a principal sponsor. When the hotel was dedicated in June 1928, Mr. Darling had reached 80, his birthday having occurred on April 22.

A big quarter-page ad in the *Caledonian-Record* of June 5, 1928 read, "DARLING INN, A Gem In The Green, Lyndonville, Vermont. Official Opening, Thursday, June 7th, A Thoroughly Modern Hotel In Every Respect, Open The Year 'Round, European Plan, Rates $2.50 to $7.00." The catch

Third from left is Herbert Hubbard; bellhop is Fernand Liberty.

PHOTO BY DON SIEBERT

A post card of the Darling Inn.

phrase, Gem In The Green, used for the hotel, was later adopted by the Lyndonville Board of Trade for promoting Lyndonville, and later became a slogan for the whole town. The tall arched windows with the small panes gave the Inn a colonial air and an abundance of light. Almost all guest rooms had private baths and all had telephones. The kitchen appliances were electrically operated, even to a potato peeler. Cooking was done on a huge coal range and charcoal broiler.

The first year the employees, under manager William C. Roberts, included a housekeeper, three maids, a parlor maid, two combination engineers and housemen, two bell hops, a night clerk, a day clerk, a head waiter or waitress, five waitresses, a chef, an assistant chef, a baker, a salad maker, two dishwashers, and a pot washer, a nice addition to employment figures.

The Inn catered to travelers, salesmen and tourists. Except for a few winters here and there when the owners thought it best to close the hotel, a few people made their permanent homes here.

The Inn was operated by the Lyndonville Hotel Company. After a series of subsequent owners, Mr. and Mrs. Andrew Janis of Manchester, N.H. opened it as the Darling Inn Convalescent Home on January 14, 1964. In 1977, when government regulations required the closing of the fourth floor, Mrs. Janis felt she could no longer run the home profitably and closed it November 19, 1978. In 1980, the building, opening as the Darling Inn Apartments had been renovated into 27 units for senior citizens by Northern Community Investment. The dining room, still with the same furniture selected by Elmer Darling, and the coat of arms over the fireplace, is the area senior meal site.

Note: I had the privilege of seeing the hotel under construction from the inside, even to the upper floors. My mother was talking to Mr. Grapes on the street who was looking over the progress of the building. He invited us to come inside so we could see it. My mother held me firmly by the hand as we climbed stairs and looked into unfinished halls and rooms—no hard hats required in those days.

Mr. Cobleigh's Gift to the People

A CEILING-HIGH STATUE of Nike, or Winged Victory[1] of Samothrace, was the first sight that met our eyes when we entered the library. It was a gift of Theodore N. Vail when the library was dedicated in 1906.

Today when people enter the library and look ahead and up a little, they see three handsome windows, each telling a story in stained glass, done by Elizabeth Robbins of Vail Hill.

In earlier days one could not speak out loud in the library. If we got to giggling or whispering too loud, Miss Angie Hunter's head would appear around the book stacks in the children's section and tell us to be quiet. Whispering is no longer a requirement in libraries, though loud talking is not appropriate.

Eber W. Cobleigh (1837-1909) had been, according to his obituary, an industrious, thrifty man who had accumulated a considerable fortune. He was listed in a Lyndon directory as a farmer with 29 acres, 300 maple trees and a Morgan stallion.

The death of his wife in 1899 and his daughter in 1904, leaving Mr. Cobleigh without family, may have prompted him to give the town of Lyndon $15,000 in 1905 to build a library that would perpetuate his name. His provisions were that it be

---

[1]The Winged Victory statue is now on permanent loan to Lyndon State College, quite appropriate since the college buildings are on land once part of Vail's Speedwell Estate.

170 **Lyndonville,** Vt. Cobleigh Public Library.

Post card postmarked 1906, the year the library was built.

built within the Lyndonville village limits, be known as the Cobleigh Public Library, that the name Cobleigh Public Library appear over the front door and a plaque be placed by the front door saying, "This building given to the Town of Lyndon, by Eber W. Cobleigh, A.D. MCMV."

The first building on that corner was George Walker's hotel built when Lyndonville was just getting started in 1866-67. It soon burned and Walker built another. It too burned in a short time. David Silsby bought the livery stable, enlarged it when business increased and rebuilt a larger one after the fire in 1894.

It was this lot that the town wanted for the library and on March 24, 1905, Silsby and his wife, Lottie, sold it to the town of Lyndon for $7,000. Silsby had to remove all buildings on the lot by June 15, 1905, because Eber Cobleigh wanted the library to be completed in the year 1906 or the money he gave would return to him or his estate.

He also gave $666.66 toward the $7,000 prime corner lot. Theodore N. Vail had contributed a third, $2,333.33. The rest came from other contributors and a town appropriation. In order to complete the building the way it was planned, Cobleigh gave another $1,500.

Cobleigh's wish to have the library completed in 1906 came just under the wire with dedication ceremonies held on December 29, 1906. In a brief speech (read for him), Eber W. Cobleigh said, "I hope that all who visit the library will feel that it is to be a place for study and pleasure and that such good will come from it in the days to come."

The building is brick with granite trimmings, plate glass windows and copper roofing. Fireproof partitions extend from the basement floor to the attic. There are brick fireplaces in the trustees room and the reading room. The interior, including the fluted columns, is quartered oak.

In 1894 the *Vermont Union* said, "This is the hottest corner in the village, two large hotels and one livery stable have gone up in smoke from that corner since 25 years ago."

Perhaps it is still the "hottest corner" in the village, but now, not because of fire, but because of all the enthusiasm of the staff and volunteers, the children's activities, the programs, the meetings and other cultural events that are constantly in progress at the library.

Even now, the library is undergoing more changes making it handicap accessible to all three levels. There will be more space in use and greater uses that can be offered at Cobleigh's gift to the town of Lyndon.

Lyndonville Station, the "Best on the Line"

B EFORE LYNDONVILLE was even named, which occurred April 13, 1868, the "new village" was already
flourishing. The railroad shops and all the other buildings
needed by the Connecticut and Passumpsic Rivers Railroad for
headquarters here, were already built or in the process of being
built on the 334.88 acres purchased in Lyndon after the railroad
shops burned in St. Johnsbury in 1866.

All this construction consisted of buildings needed for all
the business of the railroad, including company houses for some
of their employees. The company laid out streets and sold lots
for private homes, with certain restrictions, such as no houses
to be built less than two stories high or less than twenty feet
from the street. The company did not want this new village
to look like a shack town such as was sometimes the case
when gold, silver, or oil discoveries, for instance, started boom
towns.

The *Vermont-Union*, the weekly newspaper at the Corner
kept up with the news from the "new village" two miles north,
and reported the progress every week.

The passenger depot, "the best on the line," was begun when
the cellar was dug in July 1867. It was 60 by 47 feet, built two
stories high of brick, and offered enough room to contain the
various offices of the railroad company. The wooden platform
was 18 feet wide and 260 feet long.

117

R. R. Station,
Lyndonville, Vt.

Lyndonville Station: Once a busy place.

An era disappeared in Lyndonville with the passing of the station. In this electronic age some of us still have the memory of the clicking sound of the telegraph system, the first thing that came to the ears as one opened the heavy station door. What dreams and unnamed longings were stirred when one viewed a huge poster proclaiming The Great Pacific Northwest by rail with a picture of a train steaming across the country. Did people really go to such far away places?

The Passumpsic Railroad, was leased by the Boston & Maine in 1887. On June 1, 1926, this line from north of Wells River was leased to, and on November 7, 1946, was sold to CPR, the Canadian Pacific Railway. The line between Wells River and Newport became the CPR Lyndonville subdivision. Many French Canadians moved into Lyndonville to work with the section gangs.

When it was almost time for a train to arrive at the passenger station, people came in for tickets and took seats to wait for the "All Aboard!" Some waited to meet someone coming on the train. The wooden seats were like chairs with arms, but connected together in rows back to back. The room was finished with matched board wainscoting. The station agent sold you your ticket behind a counter with an iron grille above it.

The rest room, finished in wood, was strange to a little girl. It was a little scary to pull the wooden handle at the end of the metal chain hanging from a wooden box about six feet above the floor where the water was stored for flushing.

At last the whistle sounded up the track, the train arrived and stopped at the platform, whooshing off steam as it waited for passengers to descend and others to climb aboard. It was a sound that I never forgot, even if I was only going to St. Johnsbury. Riding on the train it was curious to see the backs of houses on the street across the river in St. Johnsbury Center, known as Centervale to the railroad and indicated as such on the little station. In those days there was also a small station at Lyndon.

In the late thirties, after a vacation at home, I could board the midnight train Sunday night at Lyndonville, change in Lowell, Massachusetts, for a local to Worcester, walk up Front Street and arrive at Becker College in time for my first morning class.

There is a special sound and rhythm, and sights not seen from the highway when riding the train, well described by John G. Saxe in his poem, "Rhythm of the Rail" that says, "Bless me, this is pleasant riding on the rail."

The Canadian Pacific had moved most of its operations to Canada and since there were no more passenger trains, the station was slated for demolition, no ifs, ands, or buts. There was the old song and dance given about the building being "structurally unsafe," when attempts were made by some groups to save the station for other uses. It has been gone for 21 years, gone, but not forgotten.

The Music Hall Debate

FOR A LONG TIME the Village Hall, or Music Hall, was the cultural center of Lyndonville. The post office now occupies the spot. Before the hall was built, there were mixed feelings in the village in 1883. Some thought it unnecessary, that it would be a large expense and a luxury.

Others, including village trustees, William H. Fletcher, Stephen Eastman, and Austin Houghton, thought it a would be an advantage to have a village-owned place where large gatherings could meet in safety and comfort. There were meeting halls upstairs in some of the blocks in the Ville and there was the Town House at Lyndon Center, but no place for such ambitious purposes as the pro-hall people thought would be good for the village, that it would call frequent audiences into the place, each leaving a little money and carrying away a good deal of advertising for the village.

"Of course voters hesitate to appropriate money for improvements," said the *Vermont Union*. "What voters seem to dread is letting go of the money. After they let go and obtain the improvement, they will not sell at any price."

Franklin Horatio Smith wrote a poem, just in fun, he said, not meant to offend anyone. The first verse goes:

> Ring the bells with might and main,
> Rouse the people dull and lazy,

120

Half the Ville has gone insane,
Half the rest are going crazy,
And they bawl, bawl, bawl, bawl,
    "Village hall!" "Village Hall!"
Up and down the streets they go,
Upon every voter call,
Striving very hard to show
How we need a village hall.

Trustees Fletcher and Eastman had purchased a hand-cranked, horse-drawn fire engine, complete with 100 feet of hose, a hose carriage, and nozzles in Franklin, New Hampshire, in June 1883, but the problem was—there was no place to house it. Now the village needed an engine house. Why not build the village hall and make a place in it for the fire engine?

The trustees were given the go-ahead at the annual village meeting in 1884, the cost not to exceed $4,000. Trustee Fletcher and N.P. Lovering visited modern public halls in New Hampshire and Massachusetts, looking for good ideas.

Music Hall, or Village Hall, postmarked 1910.

The hall, begun right away, was a large wooden structure 50 x 90 feet. The three trustees directed the work, with Fletcher as chief designer, and Houghton as boss of the workmen.

At the front of the building, facing Broad Street, one went up ten or a dozen steps to double doors leading into an anteroom. Two doors led into the main hall and two sets of wide stairs, one at each end of the anteroom, led up to the balconies.

The balconies were ornate with wood and iron railings that curved gracefully outward, enough to allow room for the knees of people sitting in the front row. The balcony at the end, facing the stage, was extended back over the entry and was reached by a series of steps from the side balconies. The balconies were self-supporting, so no posts were needed underneath to the floor, leaving the whole floor free for dancing, roller skating, bazaars and even donkey basketball! Also Fletcher had invented seats that were comfortable, attached in rows, so that a whole row at a time could be pushed beneath the balcony at the back end of the hall. I remember one donkey basketball game in which Kermit Grant and others, kept us in stitches all evening. At one point "Shorty" Ramsdell had trouble with the donkey he was riding. Shorty just put his feet on the floor and the donkey walked out from under him.

The basement held a kitchen, dining room, police room, two lock-ups, wood room, furnace room, water closets and the fire engine room. At times the lock-ups held those who needed over night sobering-up.

The main hall was 50 x 60 feet. The stage was 3 feet above the floor, with footlights, an arch for drop curtains, and space in the rear for sliding in scenery. There were dressing rooms beyond each end of the stage.

The Village Hall was dedicated on August 7, 1884. The entertainment, by the Boston Opera company, was a grand concert and the second act of the opera "Martha" with players "in splendid costume."

Gatherings and entertainment included musicals, concerts, lectures, conventions, plays, dances, balls (A Washington's Birthday ball was held each year for fifty years, bazaars, basketball, roller skating, movies, graded school, and Lyndon Institute graduations, including my own with Vermont Governor George D. Aiken as our speaker. People came from Boston to direct local talent in plays and musicals. There were minstrel shows before they offended anybody. Everybody just had a lot of fun. There were union services on Memorial Day Sunday (the Sunday before Memorial Day). The Lyndonville Military Band held indoor concerts in winter. The Village Improvement Society which used the building for many fund raising activities, built a portico over the front steps.

Automobiles were considered responsible, in great part anyway, for the eventual lack of interest in the cultural events and entertainment in Music Hall. The state of Vermont rented the hall for use by Company C of the National Guard, and the split-level basement continued to be the offices and stockroom of the Lyndonville Electric company.

The village bought the Gem Theater on Elm Street and it was converted to an armory. The village hall was remodeled, another floor added at balcony level, and the two floors leased to the Vermont Shoe Company in 1953. On October 23, 1954, the hall that had seen so much activity for so many years, burned to the ground. It was said that a glue pot, used in the shoe manufacturing, had been left on all night, causing it to overheat and start the fire.

In today's law suit-oriented society, the large wooden building would have been considered a detriment, unsafe, and impossible to insure. But for many years it served as a social center for Lyndonville and the surrounding area.

Here Comes the Band!

L YNDONVILLE IS ONE PLACE where you can still enjoy an old fashioned outdoor band concert in the park. You will hear waltzes, show tunes, perhaps an overture, Dixieland, and the good old rousing marches from the Lyndonville Military[1] band while the fountain splashes merrily nearby. Before it gets dark you might look to the west and see a gorgeous sunset. Children run through the park, around the bandstand, and around the rim of the fountain pool. What matter if a foot slips in the water. It is part of the fun of band concert night!

Cotton candy is available at the concerts, but looking back to the thirties and forties or so, just before time for the concert to begin, a familiar figure could be seen pushing a two-wheeled cart along Depot Street, heading for the park. It was the Popcorn Man, Joseph Beauchesne. The corn was popped over a gas flame inside the glass compartment. The popped corn was scooped into a paper bag for five cents a bag. A metal pot like a teapot with a long spout, was suspended near the flame to keep butter melted. It was simply tipped above the bag to douse the popcorn with real old-fashioned butter. The salt shaker was handy, too. Nobody told us that butter and salt were bad for

---

[1]The band no longer uses the military title, but is known as the Lyndonville Band, or Lyndonville Town Band.

Memorial Day 1940. The Lyndonville Military Band marching along Depot Street, led by drum major Ralph Hovey.

us, so in our ignorance we enjoyed every bite. Often the Popcorn Man, with his ready smile, could be found at other times stationed by the Squires and Lincoln store (now the Lyndonville Fruit store). Sometimes a church or the Village Improvement Society might have a "strawberry ice cream social" for a fundraiser on a band concert night. Dishes of ice cream were topped with a generous helping of strawberries.

As long ago as 1868, we find reference to a Lyndon Railroad Band, later a Lyndon Cornet Band, and a Lyndon Brass Band. Our former Lyndon town historian, Dr. Venila Shores, found evidence that the Lyndonville Band was organized April 14, 1869, and was ready for whatever occasion it was needed.

In 1898, the band accompanied the Grand Army of the Republic to its encampment in Cincinnati, then in other years

Concert in the park. Gerry Aubin on euphonium, Paul Aubin on trombone.

to Montreal, Minneapolis, Denver, and other faraway cities, earning the addition of "Military" to its title, and it said so on the bass drum—"Lyndonville, Vt. Military Band, Dept. G.A.R." On the GAR trip to Salt Lake City in 1909, Alphonse Aubin took his bride and made it their honeymoon. Also on this trip LMB had the distinction of being the first band to play in the Mormon Tabernacle. The band also accompanied the Masons, the Vermont National Guard, and other groups, to conventions and meetings.

Homer Wilson was the director almost continuously from 1888 to 1937, then Perley Harris directed until 1963. Other directors have been longtime members, namely John Norris and Roy Christophersen, also members Deanna Wheeler and Gary Aubin.

Alphonse Aubin's son, Paul, had played trombone in the band for 66 years when he died in 1992. Paul's brother, Gerald, usually playing euphonium, has more than 65 years, and several younger Aubin family members play in the band too.

Through these many years the Lyndonville Military Band has played for many occasions here and elsewhere, including old time minstrel shows, the Caledonia County Fair, parades, dedications, and when the Vermont Tap and Die won the Army and Navy E for Excellence, for example. Winter indoor concerts were given in 1939 and 1940 at Music Hall to raise funds for new uniforms, the old ones having become badly worn. Until the new snappy green uniforms with gold braid finally came, we wore white shirts and pants with black bow ties.

Band leader, Perley Harris.

One outstanding event was in 1941, when Vermont's Sesquicentennial was celebrated with "great pageantry" in Montpelier. Our new uniforms showed off well. Tall, slim Ralph Hovey in his drum major uniform cut a fine figure marching ahead of the band. The Lyndonville Military band "copped first prize in the band class," said the *Caledonian-Record* of Aug. 30, 1941. We worked for that honor. Every rehearsal night all summer we not only practiced our music as usual but our director Perley Harris had us out on the park marching and counter-marching, practicing over and over for this big event.

In recent years it has become harder to get people committed, especially young people—but enough get together, some from St. Johnsbury, to continue the concerts. It still adds up to summer fun evenings in Lyndonville on Wednesday nights. If you sit in your car, be sure to blow your horn when a number is done—the players consider it their applause.

Chautauqua Brought Culture

FROM 1915 TO 1933, although perhaps not every year between, Redpath Chautauqua came to Lyndonville. Chautauqua boosters—local people under the direction of an advance Chautauqua person—touted the merits and fun of Chautauqua and promoted the advance sale of tickets. A guarantee was required if Chautauqua was to come.

Redpath Chautauqua brought a week of affordable culture and entertainment to people in an era when there was no radio, at first, and no television. Though there were sometimes musicals, plays, concerts, and films in town, Chautauqua offered a great variety all in one week. The last time it came to town I was old enough to have a season pass to attend everything.

The tent raising on the Darling meadow at the foot of Main Street, was a show in itself. I remember the slap, slap sound of boards being put in place for benches, and the snapping sound of wooden folding chairs being set up for reserve seats. All this spelled excitement for kids hanging around to watch everything being made ready for the shows.

During the performances bright August sunshine filtered through the canvas tent. Electric lights were strung around for the evening performances. Morning shows were for the children. They loved the comedy piano performance by Charles Ross Taggart, something like Victor Borge does today. At one show a girl, picked from the audience to assist a magician, wound

PHOTO BY BESS NELSON, 1915

Redpath Chautauqua tent on Center Street. Charles Darling's Barn was used for dressing rooms.

Chautauqua boosters: Maude Wakefield, center, Bess Nelson, right.

up with a lap full of candy kisses, much to the envy of the rest of us.

In a letter to a friend, Miss Dorothy Walter of Riverside gave an enthusiastic account of that first exciting Chautauqua in Lyndonville. The letter, dated August 14, 1915, is an insight to what professional entertainment meant to many people in those days.

Bubbling with enthusiasm, Miss Walter wrote, "My dear Margaret . . . I wish you could have been here to go to Chautauqua with us and see how breathless the Walter family was for seven days." Miss Walter's father, Charles T. Walter, was publisher of the newspaper, *The St. Johnsbury Republican.* The press tickets he received were put to good use as Miss Walter explains:

"Bess (Miss Walter's sister) and I were the record makers of the family. We went every afternoon and evening for six days and once Sunday morning. As he (Papa) couldn't be there much afternoons, we took someone who wouldn't be likely to get interested otherwise. Don't you think that was a good use to put advertising tickets to? Several of those whom we took were folks you wouldn't expect to be interested in the best music and lectures, have said most emphatically that next year they will have season tickets of their own and go to everything. That pleases me, for it means that the Chautauqua idea is working out as it ought to do to be truly democratic.

"I am like all the rest of the people in Lyndonville, Orleans, Hardwick, and other towns that have been having the meetings; I can't talk of anything else!

"The first day there were brief addresses of welcome by citizens (of Lyndonville) and people of the troupe. The first evening Dr. Edward Amherst Ott of Chicago lectured on community building, the central idea of the Chautauqua. He spoke of what a benefit it would be to a town to have a department of the local board of trade to confer with young men and women ready to go into business and to tell them whether the town needed another lawyer, or dentist, or doctor or merchant, and to point out the way to jobs that did need doing. That struck me as a good idea.

"The next day the preludes were given by the Aida quartet, a group of young ladies. An opera singer, C. Pol Plancon, sang a song which Bess says is called 'Lo, the factotum' from 'The Barber of Seville.' The song was not really suited to the concert stage, and it sounded funny. Bess says it is intended to be a funny one, but the man didn't seem to be very much pleased when the little folks on the front seats roared and laughed.

"One evening the program was a Shakespeare play, 'Much Ado About Nothing' which was done without scenery, but the plays as Shakespeare meant them to be played, with no breaks at all. They have money to put into costumes on account of not lavishing it on scenery. The best of it is that they are all good.

"The last day Mr. J. S. Knox, a president of a business college, gave a fine talk on community building from the business point of view. He also gave me some fine ideas on teaching English, especially oral composition. Don't you think that it would be fun and good practice to have a class pretend that they were each an agent for some commodity and try to sell that to a single member of the class in the presence of the rest? That is one idea that was an off shoot in my own mind from one of the remarks he made in his lecture.

"The last evening was taken up by Mr. Bingham, such a funny man that the audience roared just to look at him. He began by saying that the other people we had heard . . . all had a message but that he was 'messageless!' Of course that started us off feeling pretty well. In spite of that though he did have a fine little message. He said that he had for his aim and ideal the giving of a whole evening of jolly fun without one indecent thing in it.

"And so ended our week of merry making. It was a real treat and very cheap at that since the season tickets were two dollars if bought before the entertainment began."

Chautauqua, just as it was meant to do, provided Miss Walter and countless others with information, new ideas, and fun for many years. Then in the early thirties, with radio and movie theaters providing entertainment and information, Chautauqua retreated down the nostalgic path called memory lane.

Swinging in the Sunset

THE SUNSET BALLROOM was a favorite place on Friday and Saturday nights for people who liked to dance. It was an era of live bands playing fox trots or two-steps, or romantic waltzes for dancing cheek to cheek.

The Corner Garage replaced the Stern and the Eaton blocks that burned in the 1924 fire. The garage owned by David (D.I.) Grapes had a distinct feature. One could drive in for gas from Broad Street and drive out on Depot Street, or vice versa.

The street level and the second story were show rooms for the new cars—Fords and Studebakers. There was a showroom on the ground floor and cars were stored and could be seen on a showroom floor upstairs as well. A big elevator out back took cars up to the second floor.

In 1930, Grapes changed the upstairs to the Sunset Miniature Golf Course. An outside metal stairway was installed at the back of the building for public use. Two and a half years later the golf course was removed and the Sunset Ballroom took its place.

The Feb. 15, 1933 *Vermont Union-Journal* reported: "Work has been going on . . . making this large hall into the most attractive and largest ballroom in this part of Vermont." It took 7,000 feet of hardwood flooring for the 65 x 85 foot room to make "one of the best [dancing] floors in northern Vermont." The platform for the orchestra had wheels and could be moved

133

PHOTO COURTESY EDWIN HOUGHTON

The newly built Corner Garage building after the 1924 fire. Sunset Ballroom was upstairs.

to any part of the hall. Scenic wall decorations, including a sunset on the west wall, a scene of Willoughby Lake on the north wall, and other scenes were painted by Gerald Flanders.

The advertisement in the *Journal* read: "Grand opening Dance of the new Sunset Ballroom, Lyndonville, Vt., Friday evening, Feb. 17, [1933]. Music by H. Guy Dunbar's famous orchestra. Admission: Gentlemen 75c; Ladies 25c." There were 160 couples in attendance, some from as far as fifty miles.

Through the years a few of the bands that played at Sunset Ballroom were Millie Beck and her dance band; Marshall Morrill and his 11-man band; Gus Westerlund and the Arcadians; Mark Andrews and The Royal Gems; Clarkie's Orchestra; Lumbra's Orchestra, and others. For a long time, Cedric (Ceddy) Sherrer and his group played for more informal Saturday night dances, with Ceddy bouncing on the piano stool as his fingers flew across the keys.

This is not Sunset Ballroom but Dunbar's Band played there every Friday night. Melvin Somers, Leo Giguere, Jack McManus, leader H. Guy Dunbar, Bob Magoon, Cedric Sherrer, and Ray McLaughlin.

Friday nights were pretty special with H. Guy Dunbar and His Versatile Band—jazzy, swingy, or sweet. He and his team could each play several instruments and would change instruments for different numbers for the effect Guy wanted to achieve. Guy himself could play 20 instruments. Sometimes he would stroll among the dancers, playing the violin on top of his head.

As the stag line gathered when the ballroom opened, the fellows would size up the unescorted girls and the girls would try not to be obvious sizing up the stag line. They could judge pretty closely by who was there about how many dances they would have. It was fun to go unescorted, except for special balls such as Washington's Birthday or New Year's Eve, because you got to dance with lots of different partners. There was no generation gap in the dancers in those days. Everyone of all ages except children, went to the dances and enjoyed dancing to the same music.

A "crystal ball" hung above the center of the dance floor. The "crystal" was actually tiny mirrors covering a round ball. As it slowly rotated, it cast moving lights on the floor and dancers near the center. The ballroom was dimly lit, but a bit brighter near the center of the room where colored lights shone on the ball to make colored glitters.

Sometime in the evening there was a surprise when during one of the dances the music stopped suddenly. The couple nearest the center under the ball received a box of chocolates and the music resumed.

D.I. Grapes' son, Clarence, managed the ballroom over the garage and the Sunset Bowling Alley under the garage for many years. Eventually he moved to Willoughby Lake to operate the Boulders dance casino, restaurant, and cabins that his father, D.I., had purchased.

The Vermont Shoe Factory had set up business in Music Hall and when it burned in 1954, the American Legion, which had been using the Sunset for meetings after the dances discontinued, gave it up so the shoe factory could move in. After the factory discontinued business there, Charles and Erma (Grapes) Lang fixed up the hall again and opened it for dances in 1958. Chet Howard and Rin Wright and other groups played then. After a few years the crowds, mostly from out of town, were more of the rowdy type and the music too loud for nearby residents, so the dances were given up.

For a long time, the First National grocery store had all of the street level except the filling station and the lubrication area (now the Green Mountain Books and Prints). The corner has been walled in and is part of the Western Auto Store.

No matter how many changes have taken place in that building, there are still many of us who remember those great evenings in the thirties and forties swinging and swaying at the Sunset Ballroom. In the summer when the ballroom windows were open, the strains of the music would drift down onto Depot Street. I am sure it called some people to come upstairs and dance.

A Gem of a Theater

I
N 1930 when the Gem Theater opened on Elm Street in Lyndonville it was, said the *Caledonian-Record*, one of the locally planned, projected and sponsored enterprises, "another consistent addition to locally financed public institutions."

In the 1920s, Lyndonville had been hard hit by the railroad shops strike, a fire (1924) that burned half of the main business street—Depot Street—and the 1927 flood that took a toll on the outskirts of the village and cut out many roads, railroad lines and crippled electric and telephone services. The Economo Garage on Elm Street had also burned in the late 1920s.

The recovery from all these setbacks brought a new look to Lyndonville in new business buildings, including a new hotel (Darling Inn) and, in 1930, the Gem Theater on the site of the Economo Garage.

Before the Gem Theater was built, silent movies were shown at the Star Theater in the Stern block on the corner of Depot and Broad Streets. I just barely remember my mother and I climbing a stairway in the Stern block to one of these silent movies. It was almost as fascinating watching the piano player whose music fitted the mood of the story as it was watching the movie. After the fire silent movies were shown in Music Hall. A red concrete star set flush in the sidewalk at Stern's Star Theater entrance, was still there many years after the fire.

138

Gem Theater, c. 1947.

Uncounted feet trod over that star even after the new Corner Garage block was built, even after the Corner Garage auto showroom became the First National grocery store, now Western Auto, Wayne's Appliances, and Lois Williams' Antiques and Collectibles. Quite some time ago the star was obliterated or covered up in new sidewalk construction.

The Gem Theater was dedicated Monday, May 31, 1930. The opening movie was "The Grand Parade," a talking, singing and dancing hit with Helen Twelvetrees and Fred Scott. During dedication week stores and businesses ran ads in the papers giving special discounts, one being Willoughby's Department Store, (clothing) which offered a ten percent discount on all merchandise purchased there during the week. Grapes' Corner Garage offered a free $235 eight-tube radio with the purchase of the first 25 used cars that week. Ice cream and sodas were on special at soda fountains at Christopher's Cafe or Edmunds' Pharmacy.

Wells and Hudson of Hanover were the architects of the brick and concrete theater that seated 500. Although Lyndonville was built long after colonial days, the Darling Inn was colonial style and the Gem Theater nearby was consistent with this style.

The 15-foot stage lent itself well to live performances. The wall of the 20-foot lobby was perfect for displaying fascinating posters of coming attractions. Posters were displayed in glass covered display cases on the outside of the theater as well. Exits were placed to ensure rapid emptying of the theater in case of emergency. The acoustical wall coverings and carpeted floors were designed to absorb sound "instead of throwing it back into the room as echoes." The rails in the back for "standing room only" were draped with heavy maroon velour to shut out any light or noise from the lobby. The speaking system was the latest R.C.A. photophone. Ushers with flashlights pointing to the floor showed people to seats if they came after a show had begun. If children even started to be noisy, someone would appear at the back and ask them to please be quiet.

John and Andrew Tegu, owners of the Palace Theater in St. Johnsbury, signed a long-term lease on the Gem Theater and signed up a long list of the leading talking pictures. Movie billboards were placed near the post office, then on Depot Street.

Children paid 10 cents until 12 years old for a Saturday afternoon double feature, a news reel, a comedy and a serial. The amber "depression glass" dishes given away on Wednesday nights have become collectors items. On nights when two could go for the price of one, kids waited in the lobby to see if some people coming in alone would let them in on the double tickets.

If a Gene Autry western with his sidekick Smiley Burnett was playing on a Saturday, my father would say to me at breakfast, "I think we ought to go see Gene Autry tonight, don't you?" I would even pass up a date in order to go to the movie with Dad.

In 1959, the Gem Theater was sold to the Masonic Fraternity after being used for a while as the National Guard Armory. Today it is privately owned and stands unused for any public functions.

Today, movies can be purchased or rented and watched in the leisure of one's own home. A push of the button and the movie can be paused so one can get a snack or answer the phone without missing any of the story. While this has great advantages it does not quite come up to the excitement of "going to the movies" in the Gem Theater when talkies first came to Lyndonville.

Trotting Park and Fairgrounds

T
HE FIRST EVENT at the Lyndonville fairgrounds occurred in 1878 when the Lyndon Trotting Park Association held a big Fourth of July celebration including horse races. The *Vermont-Union* reported that the weather was perfect, 3,000 people attended, and the Association took in $1,200.

It was 1877 when a group of stockholders formed the Lyndon Trotting Park Association. Robert Pettigrew was leading promoter, generous supporter and president of the association. Twenty acres were leased from the Charles Folsom farm, a judges stand and a grandstand erected, and a one-half mile track made.

In 1880, there was a wrestling match between a professional wrestler and a farmer. The crowd was delighted when the Vermont farmer won. In 1887, a woman called Carlotta made a balloon ascension and landed safely, though as reported, "considerably disordered as to wardrobe!"

Special trains brought in crowds—it is said the crowds ran from 2,000 to 6,000—until about 1888, when for some reason the celebrations were discontinued.

A new organization, the Northern Caledonian Fair Association was formed in 1889 and leased the grounds from the Lyndon Trotting Park Association. Fairs were held with excellent exhibits, good races, and programs of entertainment.

Caledonia County Fair.

In 1890, a surprise parade was led by the band, followed by stallions, Percherons, mares, colts, cattle, a few bulls, and 50 yoke of oxen and steers. The exhibits, entertainment and trotting races were considered excellent.

Side show attractions in 1890 included a wild woman, reptile show, snake eater, a horse freak, and "dancing girls of heavy weight." In 1902, Carrie Nation made a speech in which she informed the crowds at the fair that God told her to smash saloons and that the first man she ever married came from Vermont and died a drunkard in the army.

A *Vermont Union* editorial in 1892 complained that fairs were no longer the old-type county fairs of previous years, and that competitive feats were replaced by balloon ascensions and professional horsemen.

Sometimes bad weather, even an occasional downpour, not only dampened the spirits of fairgoers, but on occasion washed out the profits for the organization as well. In 1902, the fairs were discontinued and the land reverted to the farm. For 30 years trees and bushes grew on the grounds, buildings fell, and the race track was all but obliterated.

In 1932, Archie Donahue began jogging his horses at the old track and Lyndonville businessmen Charles Willoughby, D.I. Grapes, C.M. Darling and others, formed the Lyndonville Community Fair Association. The 20 acres of ground were purchased from Ed Lang, owner of the former Folsom farm. Everything was made ready for a fair that year.

St. Johnsbury had given up the Caledonian County Fair that had been held there since about 1851. In 1938 the Lyndonville Community Fair Association discontinued their fairs, and changed to Caledonia County Fair Association. This fair has been held here every since.

In 1955, the Mountain View Park sign was erected over the main gate, dedicated to the memory of longtime fair president Charles Willoughby, who had called the grounds by that name.

Even today, with all that goes on to keep people entertained, the fair retains an old traditional flavor of competition with showing of livestock and floral hall exhibits of produce, canned and baked goods, flowers, plants, and handiwork.

The oldest tradition of all still has a place at the fair, the one for which the grounds were developed in the first place back in 1878, the old-fashioned harness races at the old Trotting Park.

Hoss Races on Main Street

M ANY YEARS AGO, people could cure the winter blahs by going to hoss races. The Lyndonville Driving Club generated much excitement right in the village on winter Saturdays, culminating with the big racing event on Washington's Birthday and a banquet at one of the hotels for the driving club members.

Lucien LeClerc, a young Canadian, came to Lyndonville in the 1890s to work for John Moulton training horses, one a bay with a Hambletonian strain named Kendall. Later LeClerc and his brother-in-law, George LaPoint, whom LeClerc joined in the meat business, purchased Kendall. To exercise the now long-idle Kendall, LeClerc hitched him to the meat delivery cart. As Kendall regained some of his old spirit, LeClerc began to let him out at upper Main Street, testing his speed down the straightaway. Railroad shop men going home for dinner at noon stopped to watch. When it came winter, the meat cart sled worked better than the wheels the cart was equipped with in summer.

Horsemen often gathered in Ed McGinnis's harness shop underneath Webb's Hotel (now the site of the Darling Inn). Talk of having races on Main Street resulted in 12 enthusiastic men forming the Lyndonville Driving Club in December of 1897. The club was chartered in 1908. Charter members were LeClerc, Roger Ladd, Doctor Brown, Everett Ruggles, Charles

"Here they come!" Crowds lined the streets for the horse races. Depot Street, on the right, was closed to traffic. The building in the center was the "Old Corner Boarding House," now the site of the White Market. Photo taken from an upstairs porch (date unknown). Printed by Jenks Studio from a glass plate.

Lee, Ed McGinnis, Charles Darling, Frank Trefren, Austin Houghton, a Mr. Perry, Peasley Randall and Dutchy Lee.

The club's aim was clean sport conducted in a gentlemanly manner. The classes of races were arranged on the plan of the Metropolitan Club of Boston, the winner of each class being moved up one class each week and the last horse being set back one class so that the contests might be as close as possible. Horsemen of adjoining towns were invited to join the races.

The club arranged with the village trustees to use Main Street, agreeing to take responsibility for policing. Houghton scraped the street with a scraper made with railroad carsills;

others shoveled the private driveways that the scraper filled as it went by. A quarter-mile speedway was measured off.

Many traditions began that first race day in December, 1907. From 2 to 4 p.m. those Saturdays, stores closed and everyone turned out to watch the races. People lined the streets by the hundreds. To the surprise of many, the winner was Everett Ruggles' bay, C.E.R., that won, not LeClerc's Kendall.

The first Washington's Birthday race, was held in 1908. It was the finale of the season and the wives and friends of the men gave them an oyster stew supper at the Masonic Hall. Thereafter a banquet, usually at one of the Lyndonville hotels, was an annual event often attended by more than 100 horsemen. Blue ribbons and silver cups were awarded, speakers and entertainment, honored guests such as Governor George D. Aiken, and music, made for gala evenings. Bets were paid off on banquet nights.

At one Darling Inn banquet, the menu was half grapefruit, pickles, old-fashioned chicken pie, fresh peas (probably shipped in from the south by refrigerated truck or train), fresh strawberry sherbet, cookies and coffee. At a banquet in the mid 40s, Bill Cunningham of the *Boston Herald* was speaker.

In 1938, an attraction of the February 22 race was one in which horses were driven by 86-year old Mr. Rugg of Lowell, Massachusetts, and Charles M. Darling, 81. "They came down the speedway in a race of four heats and then were at the evening banquet as fit and lively as any present," said John Chase in the *Vermont-Union Journal*.

Horses' names that became familiar at the races included Eddie Volo, Lucy D., Nina Dillon, Silver Direct, Sonny Volo, Candy Express, Alma Dillon, F.E.W., Speedwell Gay, Dolly Volo, and Harvest Queen.

Some later drivers or owners—not all owners drove their own horses—were Norman Healy, Archie Donahue, Gus Bishop, Frank Carr, Ted Lawson, George Drew, Clifton Drew, Forrest Grapes, Dean McDowell, Leo Hebert, Alfred Darling,

Donald Bean, Harold Stone, Ed Stone, Perley Grant, Murray Learmouth, Percy Lynaugh, Charles Willoughby, and many others.

In later years, when the streets were plowed regularly for auto traffic, the street had to be snowed, watered by the fire department, and after frozen, it was scraped just enough to take off rough places. During race time, the side streets were roped off to keep anyone from entering the raceway.

The races continued for more than 40 years, but in later years some of them took place on the fairgrounds track or on Courser's large meadow at upper Main Street. Icing Main Street began to pose problems with auto traffic increasing through the years. People wanting to continue north or south from Lyndonville would have to drive their cars around Lyndon Center during race time. The club was responsible for putting the street back in as good a condition as possible after the races—no easy task.

On Washington's Birthday, 1963, there was an attempt to revive the sport of horse racing on Main Street. It was sub zero weather and after a couple of heats the drivers took the horses back to their stables saying it was too cold and the street too slippery.

Thus ended for sure a most unique feature for which Lyndonville was noted and which had called attention from the Boston papers, *Life Magazine*, and received other widespread notice. The early horses raced were work animals during the week and track stars on race day.

In 1938, John Chase wrote, "It has brought many people into the village through the winter, made lively days and given people an opportunity to enjoy this great outdoor sport of horse racing. The success the club has had speaks well for its management and for the cooperation received from the people of the town."

What Does the Future Hold?

B
Y NOW, according to the picture, we should be able to take a trolley around Lyndonville (even if it is spelled Lyndenville), or a bus for sight-seeing. We could take an elevated train to Wheelock and Sheffield, or a dirigible to Burke Mountain. According to the station, lower left, we could take the subway to St. Johnsbury.

This is an artist's conception of Lyndonville in the future. It was apparently drawn from a post card showing the exact same scene except for the "future" conveyances. In the picture of the future there are still horse drawn vehicles as in the original post card. Does that mean that the artist did not envision the automobiles and trucks that would fill the streets, or simply ignored the possibility in favor of a less cluttered and more pleasing picture?

The post card of the original picture (without the future drawings) was post marked 4:30 p.m., March 2, 1910, and fitted with a one-cent stamp. The card of the future is post marked 5:30 p.m., July 6, 1909.

It was a popular ploy of the day to use a post card view of a village street, add these little touches and label the card "in the future." The message on the card postmarked 1910 and showing the original scene, says: "I have marked the block that burned Monday night." The building marked is the light-colored building on the left, next to the subway station. A different post

PUBLISHED BY F. E. DWINELL

An old post card depicting Lyndonville "in the future."

card showing the front of that building says "G.B. Allyn, furniture, caskets, wallpaper, pianos."

The trolley, subway, bus, dirigible and elevated train did not materialize in Lyndonville and are not mentioned in the town plan. For the most part, people come and go on their own horsepower, however many it is, under the hood.

Harriet Fletcher Fisher

About the Author

H ARRIET FLETCHER FISHER, tenth generation New Englander, fourth generation Vermonter, was born on the Fletcher family farm in Lyndon. Her great grandparents of Massachusetts came to the Lyndon farm in 1839. She feels she understands herself and what makes her tick because of knowing the history of the area and her family—English and Scottish on her father's side, some Abenaki and French on her mother's.

Harriet graduated from a one-room school, Lyndon Institute, and Becker College, and has taken courses at Lyndon State, and Community colleges.

She has written feature stories for various newspapers since 1961. Her work has also appeared in *Yankee Magazine*, *Window of Vermont* (no longer in existence), *The Magazine of Northern New Hampshire*, anthologies *Vermont Voices* and *Vermont Voices II*. Her book, *Willoughby Lake, Legends and Legacies*, is in its fourth printing.

She is a member of the League of Vermont Writers, Vermont Historical Society, several local historical societies, and the First Congregational Church of Lyndonville. She serves on the Lyndon Town Historical Advisory Committee; is co-editor with Virginia Downs, of the *Lyndon Legacy*, the Lyndon Historical Society newsletter.

She married Paul Fisher of Lyndon in 1942 and they raised three children before his death in 1977. She has seven grandchildren and two great grandchildren.

She is currently working on another book of collected writings.